RIDING THE WAVES OF CULTURE
Understanding Diversity in Global Business

Fons Trompenaars

IRWIN
Professional Publishing®
Chicago • London • Singapore

To my parents.

First published in Great Britain by The Economist Books,
25 St. James Street, London SW1A 1HG

Senior sponsoring editor:	Cynthia A. Zigmund
Project editor:	Rebecca Dodson
Production manager:	Ann Cassady
Interior designer:	Larry J. Cope
Cover designer:	Tim Kaage
Art coordinator:	Heather Burbridge
Compositor:	Bookmasters, Inc.
Typeface:	11/13 Palatino
Printer:	Arcata Graphics/Kingsport

Library of Congress Cataloging-in-Publication Data

Trompenaars, Fons.
    Riding the waves of culture : understanding cultural diversity in
business / Fons Trompenaars.
        p.   cm.
    Includes index.
    ISBN 0-7863-0290-9
    1. Comparative management.   2. Management—Cross-cultural studies.
3. Corporate culture—Cross-cultural studies.   4. Social values—
Cross-cultural studies.   5. Intercultural communication.
I. Title.
HD30.55.T76   1994
658.4–dc20   93–48785

Printed in the United States of America
 5 6 7 8 9 0 AGK 1 0 9 8 7 6 5

Acknowledgments

This book took over ten years to complete. Many people whose paths I crossed during that time were very helpful. I would like to do justice to them all in chronological order, since I have a sequential approach to time.

I am deeply indebted professionally to Frits Haselhoff for his insights into management and strategy. He also helped me to obtain a scholarship and to defend my PhD thesis in Philadelphia. Thanks also to Geert Hofstede who introduced me to the subject of intercultural management. We do not always agree, but he has made a major contribution to the field, and was responsible for opening management's eyes to the importance of the subject.

Thank you, too, Erik Bree, Albert Schipperijn, Paul Wollrabe, and Rei Torres from the Royal Dutch/Shell Group for your sponsorship, both in money and in research opportunity during the difficult first years of my project.

I am also very grateful to the two gurus in my professional life. First of all Hasan Ozbekhan, who taught me the principles of systems theory in such a profound and stimulating way that most of the thoughts on which this book is based are drawn directly from his excellent mind. Thank you, Hasan. Second, Charles Hampden-Turner, who helped me to develop thinking about culture as a way of solving dilemmas. His creative mind encourages me continuously to stretch existing ideas to new levels. He made a major editorial contribution to this book, while always respecting what I was trying to communicate. Thank you, Charles.

I am very much obliged to Giorgio Inzerilli for his solid—at times provocative—translations from deep anthropological thinking to management applications. His way of communicating the link between practice and concept has been very important not only to this book but also to the way my colleagues and I present workshops. Many of the examples used are directly or indirectly due to him, and he also put me on the track of defining the seven dimensions of culture. Thank you, Giorgio.

I am grateful to David Wheatley for help in developing more effective relationships with clients. David is one of the few people I trust to make presentations on major points of this book without feeling too anxious.

Many thanks to my colleagues in the Centre for International Business Studies, Oscar van Weerdenburg, Leonel Brug, and Eveline Vermeulen, for their continuous support and positive criticism.

Thank you also Marleen Dekker (for swift translation), Kevan Hall (for the text on circular dilemmas), Ronnie Vansteenkiste (for many quotes), Vincent Bakker (for the important first steps of the text), Peter Woolliams (for the development of the interactive computer programs), and Bill Daniels (for the development of the Train the Trainer program).

I also want to thank Irwin Professional Publishing and The Economist Books, which published the original edition, for their support, in particular Sarah Child and Lisa Adent, who did more than might be expected of editors.

Finally, thank you Cens, Lisa, Faye, and Gaia for your patience with me.

Fons Trompenaars
Autumn 1992

Contents

List of Figures

Chapter One

An Introduction to Culture

This book is about cultural differences and how they affect the process of doing business and managing. It is not about how to understand the French (a sheer impossibility) or the British (try, and you will soon give up). It is my belief that you can never understand other cultures. Those who are married know that it is impossible ever completely to understand even people of your own.

I became interested in this subject before it grew popular because my father is Dutch and my mother is French. It gave me an understanding of the fact that if something works in one culture, there is little chance that it will work in another. No Dutch management technique my father tried to use ever worked very effectively in my French family.

This is the context in which I started wondering if any of the American management techniques and philosophy I was brainwashed with in eight years of the best business education money could buy would apply in the Netherlands, where I came from, or indeed in the rest of the world.

I have been studying the effect of culture on management for many years. This book describes much of what I have discovered. The different cultural orientations described result from 15 years of academic and field research. Many of the anecdotes and cases in the text have come up in the course of about 900 cross-cultural training programs I have given in 18 countries. The names of the companies used in most of the cases are disguised.

Apart from the training program material, 30 companies, with departments spanning 50 different countries, have contributed to the research. The countries named in the text and figures are the political entities (East and West Germany, Russia, Yugoslavia) that existed at the time data was gathered. The companies include AKZO,

AT&T, BSN, Eastman Kodak, Elf Aquitaine, Glaxo, Heineken, ICI, Lotus, Mars, Motorola, Philips, Royal Dutch Airlines KLM, the Royal Dutch/Shell Group, TRW, Van Leer, Volvo, and Wellcome, to name a few. In order to gather comparable samples, a minimum of 100 people with similar backgrounds and occupations were surveyed in each of the countries in which the companies operated. Approximately 75 percent of the participants belong to management (managers in operations, marketing, sales, and so on), while the remaining 25 percent were general administrative staff (typists, stenographers, secretaries). The database now numbers 15,000 participants. The empirical results are, however, just an illustration of what I am trying to say.

This book attempts to do three things: (1) dispel the notion that there is one best way of managing and organizing; (2) give readers a better understanding of their own cultures and cultural differences in general, by learning how to recognize and cope with them in a business context; and (3) provide some cultural insights into the global versus local dilemma facing international organizations. Possibly the most important aspect of the book is the second of these. I believe understanding our own culture and our own assumptions and expectations about how people "should" think and act is the basis for success.

This book does not attempt to be country specific. For readers interested in applications of the model described in this book to France, Germany, USA, Japan, Sweden, UK, and the Netherlands, reference is made to Charles Hampden-Turner's book, *The Seven Cultures of Capitalism*, which he wrote with my help.[1]

Finally, since the research for this book was done on Eastern and Western Germany, and their respective cultures have remained virtually unchanged, we have decided to treat them separately. While we do recognize, of course, that Eastern and Western Germany are now one country legally, culturally they still remain distinct. All references to Russia are, indeed, for Russia and are not to be confused with the Commonwealth of Independent States.

THE IMPACT OF CULTURE ON BUSINESS

Take a look at the new breed of international managers, educated according to the most modern management philosophies. They all know that in the SBU, TQM should reign, with products delivered JIT, where CFTs distribute products while subject to MBO. (SBU = strategic business unit; TQM = total quality management; JIT = just-in-time; CFT = customer first team; MBO = management by objectives.)

But just how universal are these management solutions? Are these "truths" about what effective management really is—truths that can be applied anywhere, under any circumstances?

Even with experienced international companies, many well-intended universal applications of management theory have turned out badly. For example, pay-for-performance has in many instances been a failure on the African continent because there are particular, though unspoken, rules about the sequence and timing of reward and promotions. Similarly, management-by-objectives schemes have generally failed within subsidiaries of multinationals in southern Europe because managers have not wanted to conform to the abstract nature of preconceived policy guidelines.

Even the notion of human resource management is difficult to translate to other cultures, coming as it does from a typically Anglo-Saxon doctrine. It borrows from economics the idea that human beings are resources like physical and monetary resources. It tends to assume almost unlimited capacities for individual development. In countries without these beliefs, this concept is hard to grasp and unpopular once it is understood.

International managers have it tough. They must operate on a number of different premises at any one time. These premises arise from their culture of origin, the culture in which they are working, and the culture of the organization which employs them.

In every culture in the world such phenomena as authority, bureaucracy, creativity, good fellowship, verification, and accountability are experienced in different ways. That we use the same words to describe them tends to make us unaware that our cultural biases and our accustomed conduct may not be appropriate, or shared.

There is a theory that internationalization will create, or at least lead to, a common culture worldwide. This would make the life of international managers much simpler. People point to McDonald's or Coca-Cola as examples of tastes, markets, and hence cultures becoming similar everywhere.

There are, indeed, many products and services becoming common to world markets. What is important to consider, however, is not what they are and where they are found physically, but **what they mean to the people in each culture.** As I will describe later, the essence of culture is not what is visible on the surface. It is the shared ways in which groups of people understand and interpret the world.

So the fact that we can all listen to Walkmans and eat hamburgers tells us that there are some novel products that can be sold on a universal message, but it does not tell us what eating hamburgers or listening to Walkmans means in different cultures. Dining at McDonald's is a show of status in Moscow, whereas it is a fast meal for a fast buck in New York. If business people want to gain understanding of and allegiance to their corporate goals, policies, products, or services wherever they are doing business, they must understand what those and other aspects of management mean in different cultures.

In addition to exploring why universal applications of western management theory may not work, I will also try to deal with the growing dilemma facing international managers known as "globalization".

As markets globalize, the need for standardization in organizational design, systems, and procedures increases. Yet managers are also under pressure to adapt their organizations to the local characteristics of the market, the legislation, the fiscal regime, the sociopolitical system, and the cultural system. This balance between consistency and adaptation is essential for corporate success.

Paralysis through Analysis: The Elixir of the Management Profession

Peters and Waterman, in *In Search of Excellence*, hit the nail on the head with their critique of "the rational model" and "paralysis through analysis." Western analytical thinking (taking a phenomenon to pieces) and rationality (reckoning the consequences before you act) have led to many international successes in fields of technology. Indeed, technologies do work by the same universal rules everywhere, even on the moon. Yet the very success of the universalistic philosophy now threatens to become a handicap when applied to interactions between human beings from different cultures.

Man is a special piece of technology, and the results of our studies, extensively discussed in this book, indicate that the social world of the international organization has many more dimensions to deal with.

Some managers, especially in Japan, recognize the multi-dimensional character of their companies. They seem able to use a logic appropriate to machines (analytic–rational) **and** a logic more appropriate to social relations (synthetic–intuitive), switching between these as needed.

When in Rome, Understand the Behavior of the Romans

In the process of internationalization, the Japanese increasingly take the functioning of local society seriously. They were not the first to observe "When in Rome, do as the Romans do," but they seem to act on this more than Westerners do. The Japanese have, moreover, added another dimension: "When in Rome, understand the behavior of the Romans, and thus become an even more complete Japanese."

In opposition to this we have our Western approach, based on American business education, which treats management as a profession and regards emotionally detached rationality as scientifically necessary. This numerical, cerebral approach not only dominates American business schools, but other economic and business faculties. Such schools educate their students by giving them the right answers to the wrong questions.

Statistical analysis, forecasting techniques, and operational studies are not wrong. They are important technical skills. The mistake is to assume that technical rationality should characterize the human element in the organization. No one is denying the existence of universally applicable scientific laws with objective consequences. These are, indeed, culture-free. But the belief that human cultures in the workplace should resemble the laws of physics and engineering is a **cultural**, not a scientific, belief. It is a universal assumption which does not win universal agreement, or even come close to doing so.

The internationalization of business life requires more knowledge of cultural patterns. Pay-for-performance, for example, can work out well in the cultures where this author has had most of his training: the US, the Netherlands, and the UK. In more collectivist cultures like France, Germany, and large parts of Asia, it may not be so successful, at least not the Anglo-Saxon version of pay-for-performance. Employees may not accept that individual members of the group should excel in a way that reveals the shortcomings of other members. Their definition of an outstanding individual is one

who benefits those closest to him or her. Customers in more collectivist cultures also take offense at the quick-buck mentality of the
best sales people; they prefer to build up relationships carefully,
and maintain them.

HOW PROVEN FORMULAS CAN GIVE THE WRONG RESULT

Why is it that many management processes lose effectiveness when
cultural borders are crossed?

Many multinational companies apply formulas in overseas areas
that are derived from, and are successful in, their own cultures. International management consulting firms of Anglo-Saxon origin are
still using similar methods to the neglect of cultural differences.

An Italian computer company received advice from a prominent
international management consulting firm to restructure to a matrix
organization. It did so and failed; the task-oriented approach of the
matrix structure challenged loyalty to the functional boss. In Italy
bosses are like fathers, and you cannot have two fathers.

Culture is like gravity: you do not experience it until you jump
six feet into the air. Local managers may not openly criticize a centrally developed appraisal system or reject the matrix organization,
especially if confrontation or defiance is not culturally acceptable to
them. In practice, though, beneath the surface, the silent forces of
culture operate a destructive process, biting at the roots of centrally
developed methods which do not fit locally.

The flat hierarchy, SBUs, MBO, matrix organizations, assessment
centers, TQM, and pay-for-performance are subjects of discussion
in nearly every bestseller about management, and not only in the
Western world. Reading these books (for which managers happily
do not have much time any more) creates a feeling of euphoria. "If
I follow these ten commandments, I'll be the **modern leader**, the
change master, the **champion**." The fallacy of the "one best way" is
a management fallacy which is dying a slow death.

Although the organizational theory developed in the 1970s introduced the environment as an important consideration, it was unable to kill the dream of the one best way of organizing. It did not
measure the effects of national culture, but systematically pointed

to the importance of the market, the technology, and the product for determining the most effective methods of management and organization.

If you study similar organizations in different cultural environments, they often turn out to be remarkably uniform by major criteria: number of functions, levels of hierarchy, degree of specialization, and so on. Instead of proving anything, this may mean little more than that uniformity has been imposed on global operations, or that leading companies' practices have been carefully imitated, or even that technologies have their own imperatives. Research of this kind has often claimed that this "proves" that the organization is culture free.

But the wrong questions have been asked. The issue is not whether a hierarchy in the Netherlands has six levels, as does a similar company in Singapore, but what the hierarchy and those levels mean to the Dutch and Singaporeans. Where the meaning is totally different, for example, a "chain of command" versus "a family," then human resource policies developed to implement the first will seriously miscommunicate in the latter context.

In this book we examine the visible and invisible ways in which culture impacts on organizations. The more fundamental differences in culture and their effects may not be directly measurable by objective criteria, but they will certainly play a very important role in the success of an international organization.

CULTURE IS THE WAY IN WHICH PEOPLE SOLVE PROBLEMS

A useful way of thinking about where culture comes from is the following: **culture is the way in which a group of people solves problems.**[2] The particular problems each culture must solve will be discussed below, but we focus first on what culture is. Perhaps it is easiest to start with this example.

Imagine you are on a flight to South Africa and the pilot says, "We have some problems with the engine so we will land temporarily in Burundi." (For those who do not know Burundi, it is next to Rwanda.) What is your first impression of Burundi culture once you enter the airport building? It is not "What a nice set of values these people have," or even "Don't they have an interesting shared system of meaning." It is the concrete, observable things like language, food, or dress.

Culture comes in layers, like an onion. To understand it you have to unpeel it layer by layer. On the outer layer are the products of culture, like the soaring skyscrapers of Manhattan, pillars of private power, with congested public streets between them. These are expressions of deeper values and norms in a society that are not directly visible (values such as upward mobility, "the more-the-better," status, material success). The layers of values and norms are deeper within the onion, and are more difficult to identify.

Regular Solutions Become Basic Assumptions

But why do values and norms sink down into semi-awareness and unexamined beliefs? Why are they so different in different parts of the world?

A problem that is regularly solved disappears from consciousness and becomes a basic assumption, an underlying premise. It is not until you are trying to get rid of the hiccups and hold your breath for as long as you possibly can that you think about your need for oxygen. These basic assumptions define the meaning that a group shares. They are implicit.

Take the following discussion between a medical doctor and a patient. The patient asks the doctor: "What's the matter with me?" The doctor answers: "Pneumonia." "What causes pneumonia?" "It is caused by a virus." "Interesting," says the patient, "what causes a virus?" The doctor shows signs of severe irritation and the discussion dies. Very often that is a sign that the questioner has hit a basic assumption, or, in the words of Collingwood,[3] an absolute presupposition about life. What is taken for granted, unquestioned reality, is the core of the onion.

National, Corporate, and Professional Culture

Culture also presents itself on different levels. At the highest level is the culture of a **national** or regional society, the French or West European versus the Singaporean or Oriental. The way in which attitudes are expressed within a specific organization is described as a **corporate** or organizational culture. Finally, we can even talk about the culture of particular functions within organizations: marketing, research and development, personnel. People within certain functions will tend to share certain **professional** and ethical orientations. This book will focus on the first level, the differences in culture at a national level.

Cultural differences do not only exist with regard to faraway, exotic countries. In the course of my research it has become increasingly clear that there are at several levels as many differences between the cultures of West Coast and East Coast America as there are between different nations (although for the purposes of this book most American references are averaged). All the examples show that there is a clear-cut cultural border between the Northwest European (analysis, logic, systems, and rationality) and the Euro-Latin (more person-related, more use of intuition and sensitivity). There are even significant differences between the neighboring Americans and Mexicans.

The average Mexican manager has a family idea of the organization. He or she experiences the organization as paternalistic and hierarchical, and, as in many Latin cultures, father decides how it should be done. The Mexican sees the American manager as overly democratic: what nonsense that everybody consults everybody. The American manager thinks in a way more consistent with the Protestant ethic than the Mexican who thinks and acts in a more catholic way. Most American managers distrust authority, while Mexican managers tend to respect it.

Nearly all discussions about the unification of Europe deal with techno-legal matters. But when these problems are solved, the real problem emerges. Nowhere do cultures differ so much as inside Europe. If you are going to do business with the French, you will first have to learn how to lunch extensively. The founder of the European Community, Jean Monnet, once declared: "If I were again facing the challenge to integrate Europe, I would probably start with culture." Culture is the context in which things happen; out of context, even legal matters lack significance.

THE BASIS OF CULTURAL DIFFERENCES

Every culture distinguishes itself from others by the specific solutions it chooses to certain problems. It is convenient to look at these problems under three headings: (1) those which arise from our relationships with other people; (2) those which come from the passage of time; and (3) those which relate to the environment. Our research, to be described in the following chapters, examines culture within these three categories. From the solutions different cultures have chosen to these universal problems, we can further identify seven fundamental dimensions of culture. Five of these come from the first category.

Relationships with People

There are five orientations covering the ways in which human beings deal with each other. We have taken Parsons's five relational orientations as a starting point.[4]

Universalism versus particularism. The universalist approach is roughly: "What is good and right can be defined and always applies." In particularist cultures, far greater attention is given to the obligations of relationships and unique circumstances. For example, instead of assuming that the one good way must always be followed, the particularist reasoning is that friendship has special obligations and hence may come first. Less attention is given to abstract societal codes.

Individualism versus collectivism. Do people regard themselves primarily as individuals or primarily as part of a group? Furthermore, is it more important to focus on individuals so that they can contribute to the collective as and if they wish, or is it more important to consider the collective first since that is shared by many individuals?

Neutral versus emotional. Should the nature of our interactions be objective and detached, or is expressing emotion acceptable? In North America and Northwest Europe, business relationships are typically instrumental and all about achieving objectives. The brain checks emotions because these are believed to confuse the issues. The assumption is that we should resemble our machines in order to operate them more efficiently. But further south and in many other cultures, business is a human affair and the whole gamut of emotions is deemed appropriate. Loud laughter, banging your fist on the table, or leaving a conference room in anger during a negotiation is all part of business.

Specific versus diffuse. When the whole person is involved in a business relationship there is a real and personal contact, instead of the specific relationship prescribed by a contract. In many countries a diffuse relationship is not only preferred, but necessary before business can proceed.

In the case of one American company trying to win a contract with a South American customer, disregard for the importance of the relationship lost the deal. The American company made a slick, well-thought-out presentation which it thought clearly demonstrated its superior product and lower price. Its Swedish competitor took a week to get to know the customer. For five days the Swedes spoke about everything except the product. On the last day, the product was introduced. Though somewhat less attractive and slightly higher priced, the diffuse involvement of the Swedish company got the order. The Swedish company had learned that to do business in particular countries involves more than overwhelming the customer with technical details and fancy slides.

Achievement versus ascription. Achievement means that you are judged on what you have recently accomplished and on your record. Ascription means that status is attributed to you, by birth, kinship, gender, or age, but also by your connections (who you know) and your educational record (a graduate of Tokyo University or Haute Ecole Polytechnique).

In an achievement culture, the first question is likely to be **"What** did you study?," while in a more ascriptive culture the question will more likely be **"Where** did you study?" Only if it was a lousy university or one they do not recognize will ascriptive people ask what you studied; and that will be to enable you to save face.

Attitudes towards Time

The way in which societies look at **time** also differs. In some societies, what somebody has achieved in the past is not that important. It is more important to know what plan they have developed for the future. In other societies, you can make more of an impression with your past accomplishments than those of today. These are cultural differences that greatly influence corporate activities.

With respect to time, the American Dream is the French Nightmare. Americans generally start from zero, and what matters is their present performance and their plan to "make it" in the future. This is *nouveau riche* for the French, who prefer the *ancien pauvre;* they have an enormous sense of the past and relatively less focus on the present and future than Americans.

In certain cultures like the American, Swedish, and Dutch, time is perceived as passing in a straight line, a sequence of disparate events. Other cultures think of time more as moving in a circle, the past and present together with future possibilities. This makes considerable differences to planning, strategy, investment, and views on home-growing your talent, as opposed to buying it in.

Attitudes towards the Environment

An important cultural difference can also be found in the attitude towards the **environment.** Some cultures see the major focus affecting their lives and the origins of vice and virtue as residing within the person. Here, motivations and values are derived from within. Other cultures see the world as more powerful than individuals. They see nature as something to be feared or emulated.

The chairman of Sony, Mr. Morita, explained how he came to conceive of the Walkman. He loves classical music and wanted to have a way of listening to it on his way to work without bothering any fellow commuters. The Walkman was a way of not imposing on the outside world, but of being in harmony with it. Contrast that to the way most Westerners think about using the device: "I can listen to music without being disturbed by other people."

Another obvious example is the use of face masks that are worn over the nose and mouth. In Tokyo you see many people wearing them, especially in winter. When you inquire why, you are told that when people have colds or a virus, they wear them so they will not pollute or infect other people by breathing on them. In New York they are worn by bikers and other athletes who do not want to be polluted by the environment.

STRUCTURE OF THE BOOK

In this book we will describe why there is no one best way of managing, and how some of the difficult dilemmas of international management can be mediated. Throughout, we will attempt to give readers more insight into their own culture and how it differs from others.

Chapters 2–8 will initiate the reader into the world of cultural diversity in relations with other people. How do cultures differ in this respect? In what ways do these differences impact on organizations and the conduct of international business? How are the relationships between employees affected? In what different ways do they learn and solve conflicts?

Chapters 9 and 10 discuss variations in cultural attitudes towards time and the environment, which have very similar consequences for organizations.

Chapter 11 discusses how general cultural assumptions about man, time, and the environment affect the culture of organizations. It identifies the four broad types of organization which have resulted, their hierarchies, relationships, goals, and structures.

Chapter 12 considers how managers can prepare the organization for the process of internationalization through some specific points of intervention. This last chapter is intended to deal in a creative way with the dilemmas of internationalization, and to repeat the message that an international future depends on achieving a balance between any two extremes.

What will emerge is that the whole centralization versus decentralization debate is really a false dichotomy. What is needed is the skill, sensitivity, and experience to draw upon all the decentralized capacities of the international organization.

What we attempt to make possible is the genuinely international organization, sometimes called the transnational, in which each national culture contributes its own particular insights and strengths to the solution of worldwide issues, and the company is able to draw on whatever it is that nations do best.

REFERENCES

1. For those with more academic interests I refer to my Ph.D. thesis, *The Organization of Meaning and the Meaning of Organization*, Wharton School, University of Pennsylvania, 1985, unpublished. Also see Hampden-Turner, C. and A. Trompenaars, *The Seven Cultures of Capitalism*, Double Day Currency, 1993.

2. Schein, E., *Organizational Culture and Leadership*, Jossey-Bass, San Francisco, 1985.

3. Collingwood, R. G., *Essay on Metaphysics*, Gateway, Chicago, 1974.

4. Parsons, T., *The Social System*, Free Press, New York, 1951.

Chapter Two

The One Best Way of Organizing Does Not Exist

However objective and uniform we try to make organizations, they will not have the same meaning for individuals from different cultures. The meanings perceived depend on certain cultural preferences, which we shall describe. Likewise the meaning that people give to the organization, their concept of its structure, practices, and policies, is culturally defined.

Culture is a shared system of meanings. It dictates what we pay attention to, how we act, and what we value. Culture organizes such values into what Geert Hofstede[1] calls "mental programs." The behavior of people within organizations is an enactment of such programs.

Each of us carries within us the ways we have learned of organizing our experience to mean something. This approach is described as phenomenological, meaning that the way people perceive phenomena around them is coherent, orderly, and makes sense.

A fellow employee from a different culture makes one interpretation of the meaning of an organization while we make our own. Why? What can we learn from this alternative way of seeing things? Can we let that employee contribute in his or her own way?

This approach to understanding an international organization is in strong contrast to the traditional approach, in which managers or researchers decide unilaterally how the organization should be defined. Traditional studies have been based on the physical, verifiable characteristics of organizations, which are assumed to have a common definition for all people, everywhere, at all times. Instead of this approach, which looks for laws and common properties among things observed, we shall look for consistent ways in which cultures structure the perceptions of what they experience.

WHAT THE GURUS TELL US

Management gurus like Frederick Taylor, Henri Fayol, Peter Drucker, and Tom Peters have one thing in common: they all gave (two are dead) the impression, consciously or unconsciously, that there was one best way to manage and to organize. We shall be showing how very American and, in the case of Fayol, how French, these assumptions were. Not much has changed in this respect over the last century. Is it not desirable to be able to give management a box of tools that will reduce the complexities of managing? Of course it is. We see the manager reach for the tools to limit complexity, but unfortunately the approach tends to limit innovation and intercultural success as well.

Studies in the 1970s, though, did show that the effectiveness of certain methods does depend on the environment in which we operate.

More recently, most so-called contingency studies have asked how the major structures of the organization vary in accordance with major variables in the environment. They have tended to show that if the environment is essentially simple and stable, then steep hierarchies survive, but if it is complex and turbulent, flatter hierarchies engage it more profitably. Such studies have mainly been confined to one country, usually the US. Both structure and environment are measured, and the results explain that X amount of environmental turbulence evokes Y amount of hierarchical levels, leading to Z amount of performance. The fact that Japanese corporations engage in very turbulent environments with much steeper hierarchies has not as a rule been addressed.

We should note that these contingency studies are still searching for one best way in specified circumstances. They still believe their universalism is scientific, when in fact it is a cultural preference. One best way is a yearning, not a fact. Michel Crozier, the French sociologist, working in 1964,[2] could find no studies that related organizations to their socio-cultural environments. Of course, those who search for sameness will usually find it, and if you stick to examining common objects and processes, like refining oil according to chemical science, then pipes will be found to have the same function the world over. If the principles of chemical engineering are the same, why not all principles? It seems a plausible equation.

Talcott Parsons,[3] an American sociologist, has however suggested that organizations have to adapt not simply to the environment but also to the views of participating employees. It has only been in recent years that this consideration of employee perceptions, and differing cultures, has surfaced in management literature.

NEGLECT OF CULTURE IN ACTION

Take the following meeting of a management team trying to internationalize a company's activities. This case is a summary of an interview with a North American human resource manager, a case history which will be referred to throughout the book. Although the case is real, the names of the company and the participants are fictitious.

The Missouri Computational Company (MCC)

MCC, founded in 1952, is a very successful American company. It develops, produces, and sells medium-size and large computers. The company currently operates as a multinational in North and South America, Europe, Southeast Asia, Australia, and the Middle East. Sales activities are regionally structured. The factories are in St. Louis and Newark, New Jersey; the most important research activities take place in St. Louis.

Production, R&D, personnel, and finance are coordinated at the American head office. Business units handle the regional sales responsibilities. This decentralized structure does have to observe certain centralized limitations regarding logos, letter types, types of products, and financial criteria. Standardization of labor conditions, function classification, and personnel planning is coordinated centrally, whereas hiring is done by the regional branches. Each regional branch has its own personnel and finance departments. The management meets every two weeks, and this week is focusing on globalization issues.

Internationalization.   Mr. Johnson paid extra attention in the management meeting. As vice president of human resources worldwide, he could be facing serious problems. Management recognizes that the spirit of globalization is becoming more active every day. Not only do the clients have more international demands, but production facilities need to be set up in more and more countries.

This morning, a new logo was introduced to symbolize the worldwide image of the company. The next item on the agenda was a worldwide marketing plan.

Mr. Smith, the CEO, saw a chance to bring forward what his MBA taught him to be universally applicable management tools. In addition to global images and marketing, he saw global production, finance, and human resources management as supporting the international breakthrough.

Johnson's hair started to rise as he listened to his colleague's presentation. "The organization worldwide should be flatter. An excellent technique for this would be to follow the project approach that has been so successful in the US." Johnson's question about the acceptance of this approach in southern Europe and South America was brushed aside with a short reply regarding the extra time that would be allotted to introduce it in these cultures. The generous allocation of six months would be provided to make even the most unwilling culture understand and appreciate the beauty of shorter lines of communication.

Finally, all of this would be supported by a strong pay-for-performance system so that, in addition to more effective structures, the employees would also be directed towards the right goals.

Johnson's last try to introduce a more human side to the discussion concerning the implementation of the techniques and policy instruments was useless. The finance manager, Mr. Finley, expressed the opinion of the entire management team: "We all know that cultural differences are decreasing with the increasing reach of the media. We should be world leaders and create a future environment that is a microcosm of Missouri."

Mr. Johnson frowned at the prospect of next week's international meeting in Europe.

Mr. Johnson knew from experience there would be trouble in communicating this stance to European human resource managers. He could empathize with the Europeans, while knowing that central management did not really intend to be arrogant in extending a central policy worldwide. What could he do to get the best outcome from his next meeting? We shall follow this through in Chapter 4.

CULTURE AS A SIDE DISH?

Culture still seems like a luxury item to most managers, a dish on the side. In fact, culture pervades and radiates meanings into every aspect of the enterprise. Culture patterns the whole field of business relationships.

I remember a conversation I had with a Dutch expatriate in Singapore. He was very surprised when I inquired about the ways in which he accommodated to the local culture when implementing management and organization techniques. Before answering, he tried to find out why he should have been asked such a stupid question. "Do you work for personnel by any chance?" Then he took me on a tour through the impressive refinery. "Do you really think the products we have and the technology we use allow us to take local culture into consideration?"

Indeed, it would be difficult for a continuous-process company to accommodate to the wishes of most Singaporeans to be home at night. In other words, reality seems to show us that variables such as product, technology, and markets are much more of a determinant than culture.

In one sense this conclusion is correct. Integrated technologies have a logic of their own which operates regardless of where the plant is located. Cultures do not compete with or repeal these laws. They simply supply the social context in which the technology operates. A refinery is indeed a refinery, but the culture in which it is located may see it as an imperialist plot, a precious lifeline, the last chance for an economic takeoff, a prop for a medieval potentate, or a weapon against the West. It all depends on the cultural context.

It is quite possible that organizations can be the same in such objective dimensions as physical plant, layout, or product, yet totally different in the meanings which the surrounding human cultures read into them. I once interviewed a Venezuelan process operator, showing him the company organizational chart and asking him to indicate how many layers he had above and below him. To my surprise, he indicated more levels than there were on the chart. I asked him how he could see these. "This person next to me," he explained, "is above me, because he is older."

In one of the exercises we conduct in our workshops, we ask participants to choose between the following two extreme ways to conceive of a company, asking them which they think is usually true, and which most people in their country would opt for.

    A. One way is to see a company as a system designed to perform functions and tasks in an efficient way. People are hired to perform these functions with the help of machines and other equipment. They are paid for the tasks they perform.

    B. A second way is to see a company as a group of people working together. They have social relations with other people and with the organization. The functioning is dependent on these relations.

Figure 2–1 (page 19) shows the wide range of national responses. Only a little over a third of French or Japanese managers see a com-

FIGURE 2–1
Which Kind of Company Is Normal?

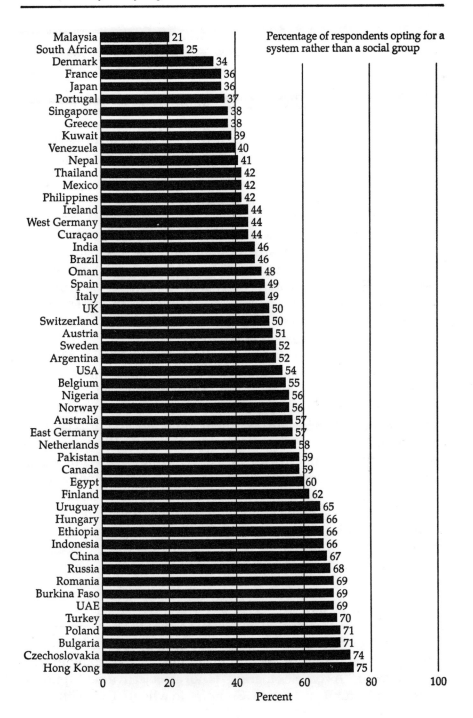

Percentage of respondents opting for a system rather than a social group

Country	Percent
Malaysia	21
South Africa	25
Denmark	34
France	36
Japan	36
Portugal	37
Singapore	38
Greece	38
Kuwait	39
Venezuela	40
Nepal	41
Thailand	42
Mexico	42
Philippines	42
Ireland	44
West Germany	44
Curaçao	44
India	46
Brazil	46
Oman	48
Spain	49
Italy	49
UK	50
Switzerland	50
Austria	51
Sweden	52
Argentina	52
USA	54
Belgium	55
Nigeria	56
Norway	56
Australia	57
East Germany	57
Netherlands	58
Pakistan	59
Canada	59
Egypt	60
Finland	62
Uruguay	65
Hungary	66
Ethiopia	66
Indonesia	66
China	67
Russia	68
Romania	69
Burkina Faso	69
UAE	69
Turkey	70
Poland	71
Bulgaria	71
Czechoslovakia	74
Hong Kong	75

Percent

pany as a system rather than a social group, whereas the British and Americans are fairly evenly divided, and there is a large majority in favor of the system in Russia and several countries of eastern Europe.

These differing interpretations are important influences on the interactions between individuals and groups. Formal structures and management techniques may appear uniform. Indeed, they imitate hard technologies in order to achieve this, but just as plant and equipment have different culture meanings, so do social technologies.

AN ALTERNATIVE APPROACH

All organizational instruments and techniques are based on **paradigms** (sets of assumptions). An assumption often taken for granted is that social reality is "out there," separated from the manager or researcher in the same way as the matter of a physics experiment is "out there." The physics researchers can give the physical elements in their experiments any name they want. Dead things do not talk back and do not define themselves.

The human world, however, is quite different. As Alfred Schutz[4] pointed out, when we encounter other social systems, they have already given names to themselves, and decided how they want to live and how the world is to be interpreted. We may label them if we wish, but we cannot expect them to understand or accept our definitions, unless these correspond to their own. We cannot strip people of their common sense concepts or routine ways of seeing. They come to us as whole systems of patterned meanings and understandings. We can only try to understand, and to do so means starting with the way they think and building from there.

Hence organizations do not simply react to their environment as a ship might to waves. They actively select, interpret, choose, and create their environments.

SUMMARY

We cannot understand why individuals and organizations act as they do without considering the **meanings** they attribute to their environment. "A complex market" is not an objective description so much as a cultural perception. Complex to whom? To an Ethiopian or to an American? Feedback sessions where people explore their mistakes can be "useful feedback" according to American management culture, and "enforced admissions of failure" in a German management culture. One culture may be inspired by the very thing that depresses another.

The organization and its structures are thus more than objective reality; they comprise fulfillments or frustrations of the mental models held by real people.

Rather than there being one best way of organizing, there are several ways, some very much more culturally appropriate and effective than others, but all of them giving international managers additional options in their repertoires if they are willing and able to clarify the reactions of foreign cultures.

REFERENCES

1. Hofstede, G., *Culture's Consequences*, Sage, London, 1980.
2. Crozier, M., *The Bureaucratic Phenomenon*, University of Chicago Press, Chicago, 1964.
3. Parsons, T., *The Social System*, Free Press, New York, 1951.
4. Schutz, A., *On Phenomenology and Social Relations*, University of Chicago Press, Chicago, 1970.

Chapter Three

The Meaning of Culture

A fish only discovers its need for water when it is no longer in it. Our own culture is like water to a fish. It sustains us. We live and breathe through it. What one culture may regard as essential, a certain level of material wealth for example, may not be so vital to other cultures.

THE CONCEPT OF CULTURE

Social interaction, or meaningful communication, presupposes common ways of processing information among the people interacting. These have consequences for doing business as well as managing across cultural boundaries. The mutual dependence of the actors is due to the fact that together they constitute a connected system of meanings—a shared definition of a situation by a group.

How do these shared beliefs come about, and what is their influence on the interactions between members of an organization? An absolute condition for meaningful interaction in business and management is the existence of mutual expectations.

On a cold winter night in Amsterdam, I see someone enter a cigar shop. His Burberry coat and horn-rimmed spectacles reveal him to be well off. He buys a pack of cigarettes and takes a box of matches. He then visits the newspaper stand, purchases a Dutch newspaper, and quickly walks to a wind-free corner near the shopping gallery. I approach him and ask if I can smoke a cigarette with him, and whether he would mind if I read the second section of his paper. He looks at me unbelievingly and says, "I need this corner to light my paper." He throws me the pack of cigarettes because he does not smoke. When I stand back, I see that he lights the newspaper and holds his hands above the flames. He turns out to be homeless, searching for warmth and too shy to purchase a single box of matches without the cigarettes.

In this situation, my expectations are not met by the individual I observed. My expectations about the behavior of the man say more about me than about him. What I expect depends on where I come from and the meanings I give to what I experience. Expectations occur on many different levels, from concrete, explicit levels to implicit and subconscious ones. I am misled not only by the meaning of the man's clothing and appearance, but also on the simple level of the newspaper and cigarettes. When we observe such symbols, they trigger certain expectations. When the expectations of the person we are communicating with meet our own, there is mutuality of meaning.

The existence of mutual beliefs is not the first thing that comes to mind when you think about culture. In cultural training workshops, I often start by asking participants: "What does the concept of culture mean to you? Can you differentiate a number of components?" In 15 years I have seldom encountered two or more groups or individuals with identical suggestions regarding the concept of culture. This shows the inclusiveness of the concept. The more difficult question is perhaps: "Can you name anything that is **not** encompassed by the concept of culture?"

THE LAYERS OF CULTURE

The Outer Layer: Explicit Products

Go back to the temporary flight detour to Burundi from Chapter 1. What are the first things you encounter on a cultural level? Most likely it is not the strange combination of norms and values shared by the Burundis (who actually consist of Hutus and Tutsis, two very different tribes) that catches your attention first. Nor is it the sharing of meanings and value orientations. An individual's first experience of a new culture is the less esoteric, more concrete factors. This level consists of **explicit** culture.

Explicit culture is the observable reality of the language, food, buildings, houses, monuments, agriculture, shrines, markets, fashions, and art. They are the symbols of a deeper level of culture. Prejudices mostly start on this symbolic and observable level. We

FIGURE 3-1
A Model of Culture

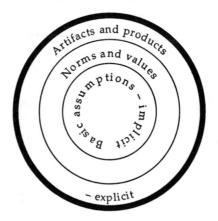

should never forget that, as in the Burberry coat example, each opinion we voice regarding explicit culture usually says more about where **we** come from than about the community we are judging.

The Middle Layer: Norms and Values

Explicit culture reflects deeper layers of culture, the norms and values of an individual group. **Norms** are the mutual sense a group has of what is right and wrong. Norms can develop on a formal level as written laws, and on an informal level as social control. **Values,** on the other hand, determine the definition of good and bad, and are therefore closely related to the ideals shared by a group.

A culture is relatively stable when the norms reflect the values of the group. When this is not the case, there will most likely be a destabilizing tension. In eastern Europe, we have seen for years how the norms of communism failed to match the values of society. Disintegration is a logical result.

While the norms, consciously or subconsciously, give us a feeling of "this is how I normally **should** behave," values give us a feeling of "this is how I **aspire** or **desire** to behave." A value serves as a criterion to determine a choice from existing alternatives. It is the concept an individual or group has regarding the desirable. For instance, in one culture people might agree with the value: "Hard work is essential to a prosperous society." Yet the behavioral norm sanctioned by the group may be: "Do not work harder than the other members of the group because then we would all be expected to do more and would end up worse off." Here the norm differs from the value.

It takes shared meanings of norms and values that are stable and salient for a group's cultural tradition to be developed and elaborated.

Why have different groups of people, consciously or subconsciously, chosen different definitions of good or bad, right or wrong?

The Core: Assumptions about Existence

To answer questions about basic differences in values between cultures, it is necessary to go back to the core of human existence.

The most basic value people strive for is survival. Historically, and presently, we have witnessed civilizations fighting daily with nature: the Dutch with rising water; the Swiss with mountains and avalanches; the Central Americans and Africans with droughts; and the Siberians with bitter cold.

Each group has organized itself to find the ways to deal most effectively with its environments, given its available resources. Such continuous problems are eventually solved automatically. *Culture* comes from the same root as the verb "to cultivate," meaning to till the soil, or, implicitly, the way people act upon nature. The problems of daily life are solved in such obvious ways that the solutions disappear from our consciousness. If they did not, we would go crazy. Imagine having to concentrate on your need for oxygen every 30 seconds. The solutions disappear from our awareness, and become part of our system of absolute assumptions.

Groups of people organize themselves in such a way that they increase the effectiveness of their problem-solving processes. Because different groups of people have developed in different geographic regions, they have also formed different sets of logical assumptions.

We see that a specific organizational culture or functional culture is nothing more than the way in which groups have organized themselves over the years to solve the problems and challenges presented to them. Changes in a culture happen because people realize that certain old ways of doing things do not work any more. It is not difficult to change culture when people are aware that the survival of the community is at stake, where survival is considered desirable.

From this fundamental relationship with the (natural) environment, man, and after man the community, takes the core meaning of life. This deepest meaning has escaped from conscious questioning and has become self-evident, because it is a result of routine responses to the environment. In this sense, culture is anything but nature.

CULTURE DIRECTS OUR ACTIONS

Culture is beneath awareness in the sense that no one bothers to verbalize it, yet it forms the roots of action. This made one anthropologist liken it to an iceberg, with its largest implicit part beneath the water.

Culture is man-made, confirmed by others, conventionalized, and passed on for younger people or newcomers to learn. It provides people with a meaningful context in which to meet, to think about themselves, and to face the outer world.

In the language of Clifford Geertz, culture is the means by which people "communicate, perpetuate, and develop their knowledge about attitudes towards life. Culture is the fabric of meaning in terms of which human beings interpret their experience and guide their action."[1]

Over time, the habitual interactions within communities take on familiar forms and structures, which I will call **the organization of meaning**. These structures are imposed upon the situations which people confront, and are not determined by the situation itself. For example, consider the wink of an eye. Is it a physical reflex from dust in the eye? Or an invitation to a prospective date? Or could it be someone making fun of you to others? Perhaps a nervous tick? The wink itself is real, but its meaning is attributed to it by observers. The attributed meaning may or may not coincide with the intended meaning of the wink. Effective social interaction, though, depends on the attributed meaning and intended meaning coinciding.

FIGURE 3–2
Culture as a Normal Distribution

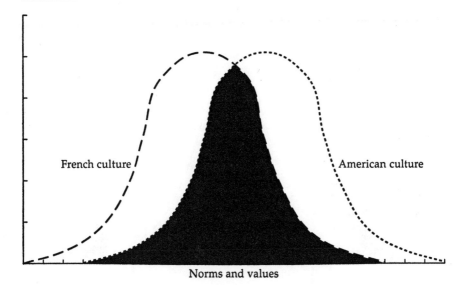

Norms and values

Cultures can be distinguished from each other by the differences in shared meanings they expect and attribute to their environment. Culture is not a thing, a substance with a physical reality of its own. Rather, it is made by people interacting, at the same time determining further interaction.

CULTURE AS A "NORMAL DISTRIBUTION"

People within a culture do not all have identical sets of artifacts, norms, values, and assumptions. Within each culture there is a wide spread of these. This spread does have a pattern around an average. So, in a sense, the variation around the norm can be seen as a normal distribution. Distinguishing one culture from another depends on the limits we want to make on each side of the distribution.

In principle, each culture shows the total variation of its human components. So while America and France have great variations, there are also many similarities. The average or most predictable behavior, as depicted by Figure 3–3 (page 28), will be different for these two countries.

FIGURE 3–3
Culture and Stereotyping

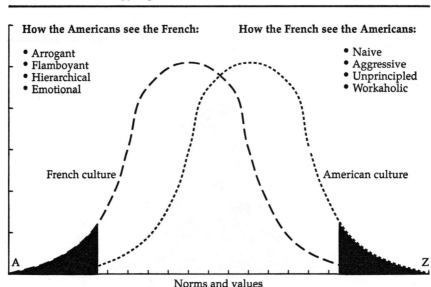

How the Americans see the French: How the French see the Americans:

- Arrogant   • Naive
- Flamboyant   • Aggressive
- Hierarchical   • Unprincipled
- Emotional   • Workaholic

French culture   American culture

A   Z

Norms and values

Cultures whose norms differ significantly tend to speak about each other in terms of extremes. Americans might describe the French as having the behavioral characteristics shown on the left side of the graph, or the tail of the normal distribution. The French will use a similar caricature for the Americans, shown on the right side of the graph. This is because it is differences rather than sameness which we notice.

Using extreme, exaggerated forms of behavior is **stereotyping**. It is, quite understandably, the result of registering what surprises us, rather than what is familiar. But there are dangers in doing this. First, a stereotype is a very limited view of the average behavior in a certain environment. It exaggerates and caricatures the culture observed and, unintentionally, the observer.

Second, people often equate something different with something wrong. "Their way is clearly different from ours, so it cannot be right." Finally, stereotyping ignores the fact that individuals in the same culture do not necessarily behave according to the cultural norm. Individual personality mediates in each cultural system.

CULTURES VARY IN THEIR SOLUTIONS TO COMMON PROBLEMS

To explain variations in the meanings organizations have for people working in them, we need to consider variations in meanings for different cultures. If we can identify and compare categories of culture that affect organizations, this will help us understand the cultural differences that must be managed in international business.

In every culture, a limited number of general, universally shared human problems need to be solved. One culture can be distinguished from another by the specific solution it chooses for those problems. The anthropologists, F. Kluckhohn and F. L. Strodtbeck,[2] identify five categories of problems, arguing that all societies are aware of all possible kinds of solutions but prefer them in different orders. Hence, in any culture there is a set of dominant, or preferred, value orientations. The five basic problems mankind faces, according to this scheme, are as follows.

1. What is the relationship of the individual to others? (relational orientation)
2. What is the temporal focus of human life? (time orientation)
3. What is the modality of human activity? (activity orientation)
4. What is a human being's relation to nature? (man-nature orientation)
5. What is the character of innate human nature? (human-nature orientation)

In short, Kluckhohn and Strodtbeck argue that mankind is confronted with universally shared problems emerging from relationships with fellow beings, time, activities, and nature. One culture can be distinguished from another by the arrangement of the specific solutions it selects for each set of problem situations. The solutions depend on the meaning given by people to life in general, and to their fellows, time, and nature in particular.

In my research I have distinguished seven dimensions of culture (see Chapter 1), also based on societies' differing solutions to relationships with other people, time, and nature. The following chapters will explain these dimensions and how they affect the process of managing across cultures.

SUMMARY

This chapter described how common meanings arise and how they are reflected through explicit symbols. We saw that culture presents itself to us in layers. The outer layers are the products and artifacts that symbolize the deeper, more basic values and assumptions about life. The different layers are not independent from one another, but are complementary.

The shared meanings that are the core of culture are man-made, are incorporated into people within a culture, yet transcend the people in the culture. In other words, the shared meanings of a group are within them and cause them to interpret things in particular ways, but are also open to be changed if more effective solutions to problems of survival are desired by the group.

The solutions to three universal problems that mankind faces distinguish one culture from another. The problems—people's relationship to time, nature, and other human beings—are shared by mankind; their solutions are not. The latter depend on the cultural background of the group concerned. The categories of culture that emerge from the solutions cultures choose will be the subject of the next seven chapters. Their significance to work-related relationships, management instruments, and organizational structures will also be explored.

REFERENCES

1. Geertz, C., *The Interpretation of Cultures,* Basic Books, New York, 1973.
2. Kluckhohn, F., and F. L. Strodtbeck, *Variations in Value Orientations,* Greenwood Press, Connecticut, 1961.

Chapter Four

Relationships and Rules

People everywhere are confronted with three sources of challenge. They have relationships with other people, such as friends, employees, customers, and bosses. They must manage time and aging. And they must somehow come to terms with the external nature of the world, be it benign or threatening.

We have already identified the five dimensions of how we relate to other people. It is easiest to summarize these in abstract terms which may seem rather abstruse. We list them again with some translations in parentheses.

1. Universalism versus particularism (rules versus relationships)
2. Collectivism versus individualism (the group versus the individual)
3. Neutral versus emotional (the range of feelings expressed)
4. Diffuse versus specific (the range of involvement)
5. Achievement versus ascription (how status is accorded)

These five value orientations greatly influence our ways of doing business and managing, as well as our responses in the face of moral dilemmas. Our relative position along these dimensions guides our beliefs and actions through life. For example, we all confront situations in which the established rules do not quite fit a particular circumstance. Do we do what is deemed right, or do we adapt to the circumstances of the situation?

If we are in a difficult meeting, do we show how strongly we feel and risk the consequences, or do we show admirable restraint? When we encounter a difficult problem, do we break it apart into pieces to understand it, or do we see everything as related to everything else? On what grounds do we show respect for someone's status and power, because they have achieved it or because other circumstances (like age, education, or lineage) define it?

These are all dilemmas to which cultures have differing answers. Part of the purpose of culture is to provide answers and guide behavior in otherwise vexatious situations.

Before discussing the fist dimension—universal versus particular forms of relating to other people—let us rejoin the perplexed Mr. Johnson of the Missouri Computational Company (MCC) from Chapter 2. He is due to preside over an international human resources meeting in which 15 national representatives are expected to agree on the uniform implementation of a pay-for-performance system. Here is some background on MCC and a summary of its main policy directives.

Since the late 1970s, MCC has been operating in more than 20 countries. As its foreign sales have grown, top management has become increasingly concerned about international coordination. Overseas growth, while robust, has been unpredictable. The company has therefore decided to coordinate the processes of measuring and rewarding achievement worldwide. Greater consistency in managing country operations is also on the agenda. There is not a complete disregard for national differences; the general manager worked in Germany for five years, and the marketing manager spent seven years in the Singapore operation.

Management has agreed to introduce a number of policy principles which will permeate MCC plants worldwide. They envisage a shareable definition of "How we do things in MCC" to let everyone in MCC, wherever they are in the world, know what the company stands for. Within this, there will be centrally coordinated policies for human resources, sales, and marketing.

This would benefit customers since they, too, are internationalizing in many cases. They need to know that MCC could provide high levels of service and effectiveness to their businesses, which increasingly cross borders. MCC needs to achieve consistent, recognizable standards regardless of the country in which it is operating. There is already a history of standardizing policies.

The reward system.   Two years ago, confronted with heavy competition, the company decided to use a more differentiated reward system for the personnel who sold and serviced mid-size computers. One of the reasons was to see whether the motivation of the American sales force could be increased. In addition, the company became aware that the best salespeople often left the firm for better-paying competitors. They decided on a two-year trial with the 15 active salespeople in the St. Louis area.

Experiment with pay-for-performance.   The experiment consisted of the following elements.

- A bonus was introduced which depended on the turnover figures each quarter for each salesperson; 100 percent over salary for the top salesperson; 60 percent for the second best; 30 percent for numbers three and four; and no bonus for the remainder.
- The basic salary of all salespeople of mid-size computers was decreased by 10 percent.

During the first year of the trial period, there were continuous discussions among the affected employees. Five salespeople left the company because they were convinced the system treated them unjustly. Total sales did not increase as a result of all this. Despite this disaster, management continued the experiment because they believed that this kind of change was necessary and would take time to be accepted.

THE UNIVERSAL VERSUS THE PARTICULAR

MCC in America is of course operating in a universalist culture. But even here a universalist solution has run into particularist problems. This first dimension defines how we judge other people's behavior.

There are two pure yet alternative types of judgment. At one extreme we encounter an obligation to adhere to standards which are universally agreed to by the culture in which we live. "Do not lie. Do not steal. Do unto others as you would have them do unto you" (the Golden Rule), and so on. At the other extreme we encounter particular obligations to people we know. "X is my dear friend, so obviously I would not lie to him or steal from him. It would hurt us both to show less than kindness to one another."

Universalist, or rule-based, behavior tends to be abstract. Try crossing the street when the light is red in a very rule-based society like Switzerland or Germany. Even if there is no traffic, you will still be frowned at. It also tends to imply equality in the sense that all persons falling under the rule should be treated the same. But situations are ordered by categories. For example, if "others" to whom you "do unto" are not categorized as human, the rules may not apply. Finally, rule-based conduct has a tendency to resist exceptions that might weaken that rule. There is a fear that once you start to make exceptions for illegal conduct, the system will collapse.

Particularist judgments focus on the exceptional nature of present circumstances. This person is not just a citizen but my friend, brother, husband, child, or person of unique importance to me, with special claims on my love or my hatred. I must therefore sustain, protect, or discount this person **no matter what the rules say.**

Business people from both societies will tend to think each other corrupt. A universalist will say of particularists, "They cannot be trusted because they will always help their friends"; a particularist, conversely, will say of universalists, "You cannot trust them; they would not even help a friend."

In practice we use both kinds of judgment, and in most situations we encounter they reinforce each other. If a female employee is harassed in the workplace, we would disapprove of this because "harassment is immoral and against company rules," and/or because "it was a terrible experience for Jennifer and really upset her." The universalist's chief objection, though, will be the breach of rules: "women should not have to deal with harassment in the workplace; it is wrong." The particularist is likely to be more disapproving of the fact that it caused distress to poor Jennifer.

Problems are not always so easily agreed upon as this one. Sometimes rules of supposed universal application do not cover a case of particular concern very well. There are circumstances much more complex than the rules appear to have envisaged. Consider the further adventures of the Missouri Computational Company, with its head office in St. Louis intent on imposing general policy guidelines on employees of many nations.

MCC has recently acquired a small but successful Swedish software company. Its head founded it three years ago with his son Carl, and his newly graduated daughter Clara and his youngest son Peter joined 12 months ago. Since the acquisition, MCC has injected considerable capital and also given the company its own computer distribution and servicing in Sweden. This has given a real boost to the business.

MCC is now convinced that rewards for salespeople must reflect the increasing competition in the market. It has decreed that at least 30 percent of remuneration must depend on individual performance. At the beginning of this year, Carl married a very rich wife. The marriage is happy, and this has had an effect on his sales record. He will easily earn the 30 percent bonus, though this will be small in relation to his total income supplemented by his wife's and by his share of the acquisition payment.

Peter has a less happy marriage and much less money. His only average sales figures will mean that his income will be reduced when he can ill afford it. Clara, who married while still in school, has two children and this year lost her husband in an air crash. This tragic event caused her to have a weak sales year.

At the international sales conference, national MCC managers present their salary and bonus ranges. The head of the Swedish company believes that performance should be rewarded and that favoritism should be avoided; he has many nonfamily members in his company. Yet he knows that unusual circumstances in the lives of his children have made this contest anything but fair. The rewards withheld will hurt more deeply than the rewards bestowed will motivate. He tries to explain the situation to the American human resources chief and the British representative, who both look skeptical and talk about excuses. He accedes to their demands.

His colleagues from France, Italy, Spain, and the Middle East, who all know the situation, stare in disbelief. They would have backed him on the issue. His family later say they feel let down. This was not what they joined the company for.

This episode from our ongoing MCC case shows that universalist and particularist points of view are not always easy to reconcile. The culture you come from, your personality, religion, and the bonds with those concerned lead you to favor one approach more than another.

UNIVERSALIST VERSUS PARTICULARIST ORIENTATIONS IN DIFFERENT COUNTRIES

Much of the research into this cultural dimension has come from America, and is influenced by American cultural preferences. The emerging consensus among these researchers, though, is that universalism is a feature of modernization per se, of more complex and developed societies. Particularism, they argue, is a feature of smaller, largely rural communities in which everyone knows everyone personally. The implication is that universalism and sophisticated business practice go together, and all nations might be better off for more nearly resembling America.

I do not accept this conclusion. Instead, I believe that cultural dilemmas need to be reconciled in a process of understanding the advantages of each cultural preference. The creation of wealth and the development of industry should be an evolving process of discovering more and better universals covering and sustaining more particular cases and circumstances.

The story below, created by Stouffer and Toby (Americans),[1] is another exercise used in our workshops. It takes the form of a dilemma which measures universal and particularist responses.

You are riding in a car driven by a close friend. He hits a pedestrian. You know he was going at least 35 miles per hour in an area of the city where the maximum allowed speed is 20 miles per hour. There are no witnesses. His lawyer says that if you testify under oath that he was only driving 20 miles per hour it may save him from serious consequences.

What right has your friend to expect you to protect him?

    1a. My friend has a definite right as a friend to expect me to testify to the lower figure.

    1b. He has some right as a friend to expect me to testify to the lower figure.

    1c. He has no right as a friend to expect me to testify to the lower figure.

What do you think you would do in view of the obligations of a sworn witness and the obligation to your friend?

    1d. Testify that he was going 20 miles an hour.

    1e. Not testify that he was going 20 miles an hour.

Figure 4–1 shows the result of putting these questions to a variety of nationalities. The percentage represents those who answered that the friend had no right or some right and would then not testify (c or b + e). North Americans and most North Europeans emerge as almost totally universalist in their approach to the problem. The proportion falls to under 70 percent for the French and Japanese, while in Venezuela two-thirds of respondents would lie to the police to protect their friend.

Time and again in my workshops, the universalists' response is that as the seriousness of the accident increases, the obligation to help their friend decreases. They seem to be saying to themselves, "The law was broken and the serious condition of the pedestrian underlines the importance of upholding the law." This suggests that universalism is rarely used to the exclusion of particularism, rather that it forms the first principle in the process of moral reasoning. Particular consequences remind us of the need for universal laws.

Particularist cultures, however, are rather more likely to support their friend as the pedestrian's injuries increase. They seem to reason, "My friend needs my help more than ever now that he is in serious trouble with the law." Universalists would regard such an

FIGURE 4–1
The Car and the Pedestrian

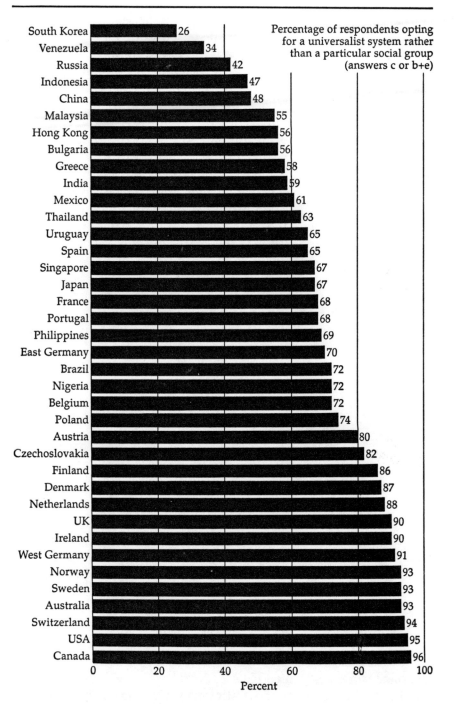

Percentage of respondents opting for a universalist system rather than a particular social group (answers c or b+e)

Country	Percent
South Korea	26
Venezuela	34
Russia	42
Indonesia	47
China	48
Malaysia	55
Hong Kong	56
Bulgaria	56
Greece	58
India	59
Mexico	61
Thailand	63
Uruguay	65
Spain	65
Singapore	67
Japan	67
France	68
Portugal	68
Philippines	69
East Germany	70
Brazil	72
Nigeria	72
Belgium	72
Poland	74
Austria	80
Czechoslovakia	82
Finland	86
Denmark	87
Netherlands	88
UK	90
Ireland	90
West Germany	91
Norway	93
Sweden	93
Australia	93
Switzerland	94
USA	95
Canada	96

Percent

attitude as corrupt. What if we all started to lie on behalf of those close to us? Society would fall apart. There is indeed something in this argument. But particularism, which is based on a logic of the heart and human friendship, may also be the chief reason that citizens would not break laws in the first place. Do you love your children or present them with a copy of the civil code? And what if the law becomes a weapon in the hands of a corrupt elite? You can choose what you call corruption.

I presented this dilemma in a workshop I was giving some time ago. There was one British woman, Fiona, among the group of French participants. Fiona started the discussion of the dilemma by asking about the condition of the pedestrian. Without that information, she said, it would be impossible to answer the question. When the group asked her why this information was so indispensable, Dominique, an employee of a French airline, interjected: "Naturally it is, because if the pedestrian is very seriously injured or even dead, then my friend has the absolute right to expect my support. Otherwise, I would not be so sure." Fiona, slightly irritated but still laughing, said: "That's amazing. For me it is absolutely the other way around."

This illustration shows that we "anchor" our response in one of the two principles. All nations might agree that universals and particulars should ideally be resolved, that is, that all exceptional cases be judged by more humane rules. What differs are their starting points.

As Figure 4–1 shows, universalists are more common in protestant cultures, where the congregation relates to God by obedience to His written laws. There are no human intermediaries between God and His adherents, no one with the discretion to hear particular confessions, forgive sins, or make special allowances. Predominantly Catholic cultures retained these features of religion, which are more relational and particularist. People can break commandments and still find compassion for their unique circumstances. God for the Catholics is like them, moreover; He will probably understand that you were lying for your friend, particularly one who had the bad luck to have the stupid pedestrian crossing in front of his or her car.

Countries with strongly universalist cultures try to use the courts to mediate conflicts. A recently released American book on automobile insurance is called *Hit Me I Need the Money*. Indeed America, credited with being the most litigious society on earth, has considerably more lawyers per person than relatively particularist Japan. The more universal the country, the greater the need for an institution to protect the truth.

There is also, incidentally, a strong correlation between universalism and expenditure per person on pet food. This is not the same as pet ownership; particularist France has more dogs than universalist Germany, but French dogs are integrated into the family and eat leftovers. It has nothing to do with what lawyers eat, either; the reason is the lack of trust in humanity in a universalist society. Dogs, like lawyers, are the institution needed for protection, and one of the ways mistrust in people can be combatted.

However, countries may be more or less universalist depending on what the rules are **about**. French and Brazilian managers, who were particularist on the traffic accident, believe that when writing on a subject as important as food, you have a universal obligation to truth. Consider the following scenario, described by Stouffer and Toby.

> You are a newspaper journalist who writes a weekly review of new restaurants. A close friend of yours has sunk all her savings in a new restaurant. You have eaten there and you really think the restaurant is no good.

> What right does your friend have to expect you to go easy on her restaurant in your review?

> 1a. She has a definite right as a friend to expect me to go easy on her restaurant in my review.

> 1b. She has some right as a friend to expect me to do this for her.

> 1c. She has no right as a friend to expect me to do this for her.

> Would you go easy on her restaurant in your review given your obligations to your readers and your obligation to your friend?

> 1d. Yes.

> 1e. No.

In this second example, a universalist's view is that as a journalist you are writing for everyone, the universe of readers, not for your friend. Your obligation is to be truthful and unbiased. In some cultures, then, it seems more important to universalize good taste than legal procedure. For them it is easier to leave the pedestrian in trouble than to judge the quality of food wrongly. (See Figure 4–2.)

FIGURE 4–2
The Bad Restaurant

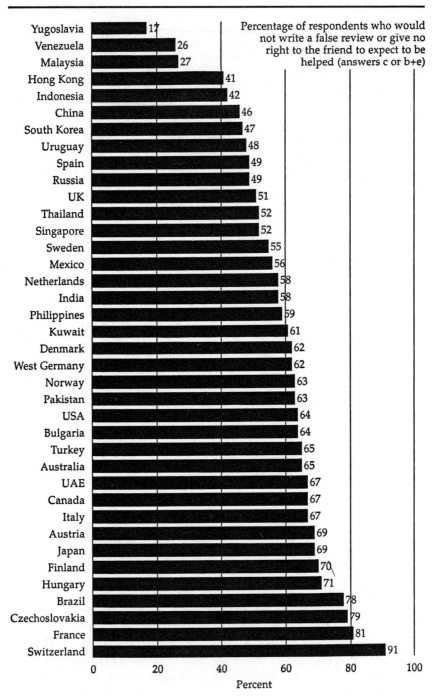

Percentage of respondents who would not write a false review or give no right to the friend to expect to be helped (answers c or b+e)

Country	Percent
Yugoslavia	17
Venezuela	26
Malaysia	27
Hong Kong	41
Indonesia	42
China	46
South Korea	47
Uruguay	48
Spain	49
Russia	49
UK	51
Thailand	52
Singapore	52
Sweden	55
Mexico	56
Netherlands	58
India	58
Philippines	59
Kuwait	61
Denmark	62
West Germany	62
Norway	63
Pakistan	63
USA	64
Bulgaria	64
Turkey	65
Australia	65
UAE	67
Canada	67
Italy	67
Austria	69
Japan	69
Finland	70
Hungary	71
Brazil	78
Czechoslovakia	79
France	81
Switzerland	91

Percent

A third dilemma I use to explore this dimension has to do with the rule of confidentiality concerning the secret deliberations of a business.

You have just come from a secret meeting of the board of directors of a company. You have a close friend who will be ruined unless she can get out of the market before the board's decision becomes known. You happen to be having a dinner at the friend's home this evening.

What right does your friend have to expect you to tip her off?

1a. She has a definite right as a friend to expect me to tip her off.
1b. She has some right as a friend to expect me to tip her off.
1c. She has no right as a friend to expect me to tip her off.

Would you tip her off in view of your obligations to the company and your obligation to your friend?

1d. Yes.
1e. No.

There are some interesting differences here between the scores on this dilemma and the previous two. The Japanese, especially, jump from the situational ethics they showed previously to a strongly universalistic stance on corporate confidentiality. Quite possibly this occurs because the situation is broader than a particular friend; at stake here is loyalty to a group or corporation versus loyalty to an individual outside that group.

This dilemma may also be presenting issues of collectivism versus individualism, to be considered in Chapter 5. As these dimensions are related as well as relational, we must be careful in interpreting the meaning different national groups give them.

UNIVERSALISM VERSUS PARTICULARISM IN INTERNATIONAL BUSINESS

When companies go global, there is an almost inevitable move towards universalist ways of thinking. After all, products and services are being offered to a wider and wider universe of people. Their willingness to buy is "proof" of a universal appeal. It follows that the ways of producing the product, managing those who make

FIGURE 4–3
Insider Information

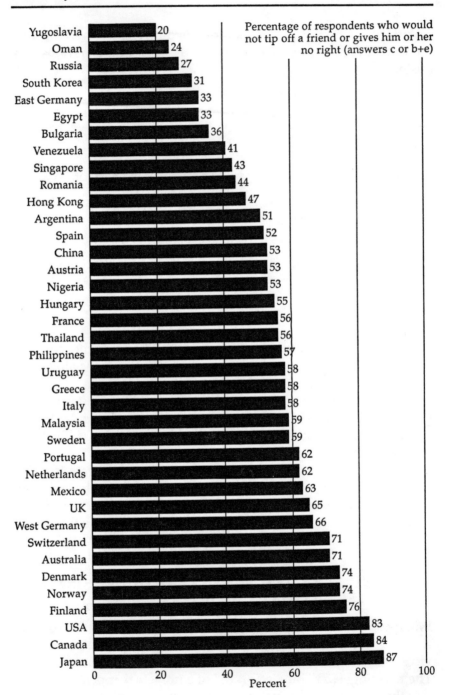

Percentage of respondents who would not tip off a friend or gives him or her no right (answers c or b+e)

Country	Percent
Yugoslavia	20
Oman	24
Russia	27
South Korea	31
East Germany	33
Egypt	33
Bulgaria	36
Venezuela	41
Singapore	43
Romania	44
Hong Kong	47
Argentina	51
Spain	52
China	53
Austria	53
Nigeria	53
Hungary	55
France	56
Thailand	56
Philippines	57
Uruguay	58
Greece	58
Italy	58
Malaysia	59
Sweden	59
Portugal	62
Netherlands	62
Mexico	63
UK	65
West Germany	66
Switzerland	71
Australia	71
Denmark	74
Norway	74
Finland	76
USA	83
Canada	84
Japan	87

Percent

it, and distributing it to customers should also be universalized. Let us consider the following examples of some of the areas where the universalist versus particularlist dilemma shows up:

- The contract
- Timing a business trip
- The role of the head office
- Job evaluations and rewards

The Contract

Weighty contracts are a way of life in universalist cultures. A contract serves to record an agreement on principle and codifies what the respective parties have promised to do. It also implies consent to the agreement and provides recourse if the parties do not keep to their side of the deal. Introducing lawyers into the process of negotiation puts the parties on notice that any breach could be costly and that promises made initially must be kept, even if these prove inconvenient.

How might a legal contract be perceived by a more particularist business partner? There is another reason why people tend to keep their promises. They have a personal relationship with their colleague, whom they hold in particular regard. If you introduce contracts with strict requirements and penalty clauses, the implied message is that one party would cheat the other if not legally restrained from doing so. Those who feel they are not trusted may accordingly behave in untrustworthy ways. Alternatively, they may terminate their relationship with a universalist business partner because that partner's precautions offend them and the contract terms are too rigid to allow a good working relationship to evolve.

One serious pitfall for universalist cultures in doing business with more particularist ones is that the importance of the relationship is often ignored. The contract will be seen as definitive by the universalist, but only as a rough guideline or approximation by the particularist. The latter will want to make the contract as vague as possible, and may object to clauses that tie them down. This is not necessarily a sign of impending subterfuge, but a preference for mutual accommodation.

Given the rise of Japanese economic power, the automatic superiority of the universalist position can no longer be assumed. Good customer relationships and good employee relationships may involve doing **more** than the contract requires. Moreover, relationships have a flexibility and durability which contracts often lack. Asian, Arab, and Latin business people may expect contracts to be qualified where circumstances have changed.

In a ten-year contract between a Canadian ball bearing producer and an Arabic machine manufacturer, a minimum annual quantity of ball bearings was agreed upon. After about six years, the orders from the Middle East stopped coming in. The Canadians' first reaction was: "This is illegal."

A visit to the customer only increased their confusion. The contract had apparently been cancelled unilaterally by the Arabs because the Canadian contract signer had left the company. The so-called universally applicable law was not considered relevant any more in the eyes of the Arabs. What could the Canadians say against this logic, especially when they discovered that the ball bearings were never even used? It turned out that the product was purchased solely out of the particular loyalty to the Canadian contract signer, not because of a felt legal obligation.

Timing a Business Trip

A universalist business person—a North American, British, Dutch, German, or Scandinavian—is wise to take much longer than usual when visiting a particularist culture. Particularists get suspicious when hurried. At least twice the time normally necessary to establish a contractual agreement is necessary to forge what has to be a closer relationship. It is important to create a sound relational and trustworthy basis that equates the quality of the product with the quality of the personal relationship. Rolls-Royce recently gave Toyota a deadline to make an acquisition offer, and Toyota promptly withdrew. This process takes a considerable amount of time, but for particularists, the time taken to grow close to your partner is saved in the avoidance of trouble in the future. If you are not willing to take time now, the relationship is unlikely to survive vicissitudes.

The Role of the Head Office

In those Western countries which are high in universalism, the head office tends to hold the keys to global marketing, global production, and global human resource management. My own experience, though, is that within more particularist national cultures, the writ of the head office fails to shape local ways of operating. Different groups develop their own local standards which become the basis of their solidarity and resistance to centralized edicts. Stratified boundaries are created by the national subsidiary between itself and the head office, and differentiation is deliberately sought.

Particularist groups seek gratification through relationships, especially relationships to the leader. Generally, the more particularist, the greater the commitment between employer and employee. The employer in these cultures strives to provide a broad array of satisfactions to employees: security, money, social standing, goodwill, and socio-emotional support. Relationships are typically close and long-lasting. Job turnover is low, and commitments to the labor force long-term. The local chief wishes all this to reflect to his or her own credit, not that of the foreign owner. Research done in an American bank with branches in Mexico found Mexican staff to be far more particularlist, with a tendency to distance themselves as far as possible from the head office in America in order to minimize universalist pressures.[2]

What frequently occurs is that foreign-based subsidiaries will pretend to comply with head office directives, which leads to a kind of ritualistic corporate rain dance. They will go through the motions so long as they are under scrutiny, but they do not believe that rain will result. As soon as the attention of the head office is diverted to other matters, normal life resumes.

Job Evaluation

Head office policies in the human resource area often lay down systems that all expatriate managers are required to apply locally. The logic of this universal system—that all jobs should be described, all candidates should have their qualifications compared with these descriptions, and all employees should have their performance evaluated against what their contracts specified they would do—is surely "beyond culture." It seems a demonstrably fair and universal way of managing.

This general system sprang up in the post-war years when companies, especially American multinationals, saw very rapid growth. Thousands of employees within America needed fair methods of appraisal and promotion, and before long this spread to the rest of the developed world. Labor unions often gave their support to these methods, seeing them as protection from arbitrary discipline or anti-union activity. A worker could only be fired for demonstrable failure to do a defined piece of work. In such regulations there was, indeed, protection for many employees. Managers had to behave consistently. They could not take harsh steps in one instance and be lenient in another.

A system designed by Colonel Hay of the American army, called the HAY job evaluation system, is now widely used in businesses to evaluate what base salaries should be for the performance of various functions. Each function and job within it is scored with the help of the employee, his or her direct superior, and a panel which includes people doing similar jobs elsewhere. This helps to maintain internal consistency and facilitates transfers between different subsidiaries throughout a company's network without changes in salary or training. Minor concessions are usually made to local conditions by way of a cost-of-living allowance, but otherwise uniformity is maintained. All this sounds highly plausible. All such procedures may appear to be working with the paperwork duly completed. But what in fact happens in more particularist societies?

The following incident occurred in a multinational oil company. During a presentation to a group of Venezuelan managers, representatives from the head office were explaining new developments in the HAY function assessment system for R&D functions. They explained that the function would be less clearly separated from the function-holder, and that there would now be benchmarks determining the level of the function. The Venezuelans showed the pro forma response by concluding the presentation with a loud round of applause.

After a good lunch and a third glass of wine, a few of the Venezuelan managers became quite talkative. They asked whether the visiting group would be interested in hearing about the Venezuelan way of assessing functions in the laboratory. "Would you like to hear what we say we do or what we really do?" they asked. Already aware of what their party line was, the head office representatives asked for what really went on.

Reality turned out to be much simpler than the complex system. Each year, they explained, the six-person management team got together after the assessment round. In the meeting, this group decided on the most appropriate candidates for promotion. The employees selected were then rushed to the human resources department in order to set up the function description required by head office. Human resources had already been informed of what the score was to be for the particular functions.

This is an interesting example of reverse causality. Instead of the job description and evaluation choosing the person that best filled it, the person was first informally and intuitively chosen, and then wrote his or her own description and evaluation.

This begs the question of whether a process in which universals guide particulars is necessarily better than a process in which particular people guide and choose their universals. As the local Venezuelan boss put it: "Who decides on the promotion of **my** subordinates, Colonel Hay or me?" The same kind of question and circularity will arise when we consider performance and achievement in Chapter 8.

RECONCILING UNIVERSALISM AND PARTICULARISM

In all the seven cultural dichotomies we have identified, of which universalism versus particularism is the first, the two extremes can always in a sense be found in the same person. The two horns of the dilemma are very close to each other, as it is easy to realize if, as a universalist, you substitute your father or daughter for the friend who is driving the car. In fruitful cross-cultural encounters, both sides avoid pathological excesses. Figure 4–4, whose methodology was devised by Charles Hampden-Turner,[3] illustrates this.

FIGURE 4–4
Reconciling Universalism and Particularism

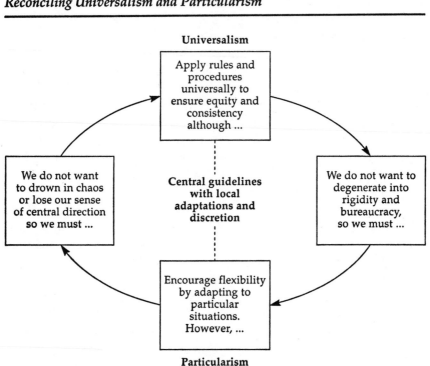

Finally we should return to Mr. Johnson of MCC.

- What do you think will happen when he tries to introduce pay-for-performance worldwide, especially in particularistic cultures?
- Do you believe that bonuses of 30 percent, 60 percent, and 100 percent over salary, taken from the salaries of other employees, will be deemed fair?
- Will high performers be encouraged or discouraged in their work by those whose salaries have been cut in order to pay them?
- Will local management cooperate wholeheartedly in this change or find ways of getting around it?
- Does local management have it in its power to organize sales territories so that it can choose who performs well for particular areas?

PRACTICAL TIPS FOR DOING BUSINESS IN UNIVERSALIST AND PARTICULARIST CULTURES

Recognizing the Differences

Universalist	Particularist
1. Focus is more on rules than relationships.	1. Focus is more on relationships than on rules.
2. Legal contracts are readily drawn up.	2. Legal contracts are readily modified.
3. A trustworthy person is the one who honors his or her word or contract.	3. A trustworthy person is the one who honors changing mutualities.
4. There is only one truth or reality, that which has been agreed to.	4. There are several perspectives on reality relative to each participant.
5. A deal is a deal.	5. Relationships evolve.

Tips for Doing Business with:

Universalists (for particularists)	Particularists (for universalists)
1. Be prepared for rational, professional arguments and presentations that push for your acquiescence.	1. Be prepared for personal meandering or irrelevancies that do not seem to be going anywhere.
2. Do not take impersonal, get-down-to-business attitudes as rude.	2. Do not take personal, get-to-know-you attitudes as small talk.
3. Carefully prepare the legal ground with a lawyer if in doubt.	3. Carefully consider the personal implications of your legal safeguards.

When Managing and Being Managed

Universalists	Particularists
1. Strive for consistency and uniform procedures.	1. Build informal networks and create private understandings.
2. Institute formal ways of changing the way business is conducted.	2. Try to alter informally accustomed patterns of activity.
3. Modify the system so that the system will modify you.	3. Modify relations with you, so that you will modify the system.
4. Signal changes publicly.	4. Pull levers privately.
5. Seek fairness by treating all like cases in the same way.	5. Seek fairness by treating all cases on their special merits.

REFERENCES

1. Stouffer, S. A. and J. Toby, "Role Conflict and Personality," *American Journal of Sociology*, LUI-5, 1951, pp. 395–406.
2. Zurcher, L. A., A. Meadows, and S. L. Zurcher, "Value Orientations, Role Conflict and Alienation from Work; a Cross-Cultural Study," *American Sociological Review*, No. 30, 1965, pp. 539–48.
3. Adapted with the permission of The Free Press, a Division of Macmillan, Inc. from *Charting the Corporate Mind:* Graphic Solutions to Business Conflicts by Charles Hampden-Turner. Copyright © 1990 by The Free Press.

Chapter Five

The Group
and the Individual

The conflict between what each of us wants as an individual, and the interests of the group we belong to, is the second of our five dimensions covering how people relate to other people. Do we relate to others by discovering what each one of us individually wants and then trying to negotiate the differences, or do we place ahead of this some shared concept of the public and collective good?

Individualism has been described by Parsons and Shils[1] as "a prime orientation to the self," and collectivism as "a prime orientation to common goals and objectives." Just as for our first dimension, cultures do typically vary in putting one or the other of these approaches first in their thinking processes, although both may be included in their reasoning. The 15,000 managers who have answered the following questions show this, although the division here is not quite so sharp as for the universal versus the particular example.

> Two people were discussing ways in which individuals could improve the quality of life.
>
> **A.** One said: "It is obvious that if individuals have as much freedom as possible and the maximum opportunity to develop themselves, the quality of their lives will improve as a result."
>
> **B.** The other said: "If individuals are continuously taking care of their fellow human beings, the quality of life will improve for everyone, even if it obstructs individual freedom and individual development."
>
> Which of the two ways of reasoning do you think is usually best, A or B?

As Figure 5–1 shows, the highest-scoring individualists are the Canadians, closely followed by the Americans, Norwegians, and

FIGURE 5–1
The Quality of Life

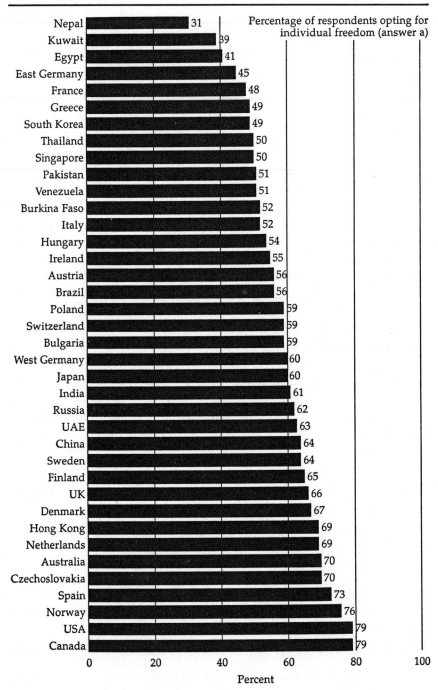

Percentage of respondents opting for individual freedom (answer a)

Country	Percent
Nepal	31
Kuwait	39
Egypt	41
East Germany	45
France	48
Greece	49
South Korea	49
Thailand	50
Singapore	50
Pakistan	51
Venezuela	51
Burkina Faso	52
Italy	52
Hungary	54
Ireland	55
Austria	56
Brazil	56
Poland	59
Switzerland	59
Bulgaria	59
West Germany	60
Japan	60
India	61
Russia	62
UAE	63
China	64
Sweden	64
Finland	65
UK	66
Denmark	67
Hong Kong	69
Netherlands	69
Australia	70
Czechoslovakia	70
Spain	73
Norway	76
USA	79
Canada	79

Percent

Spanish, all over 70 percent in favor of A. Some of the lowest-scoring Europeans are the French at 48 percent. This may come as a surprise. But remember that the French take all vacations in August, on the same date. They join the Club Méditerranée in order to be together. In the Netherlands we spread our holidays dates (otherwise we might meet one of our relations). For the French, the collectivity is France and the family. They become individualists in other social encounters. That the Japanese are significantly more individualist in their answers to this question than the French is particularly interesting; also that the Chinese score, though only slightly, as more individualist than the Japanese.

CONCEPTS OF INDIVIDUALISM AND COLLECTIVISM

Individualism is often regarded as the characteristic of a modernizing society, while collectivism reminds us of both more traditional societies and the failure of the communist experiment. We shall see, though, that the success of the "Five Dragons"—Japan, Hong Kong, Singapore, South Korea, and Taiwan—raises serious questions about both the success and the inevitability of individualism.

As in the case of universalism and particularism, it is probably truer to say that these dimensions are complementary, not opposing, preferences. They can each be effectively reconciled by an integrative process, a universalism that learns its limitations from particular instances, for example, and by the individual voluntarily addressing the needs of the larger group.

International management is seriously affected by individualist or collectivist preferences within various countries. Negotiations, decision making, and motivation are the most critical areas. Practices such as promotion for recognized achievements and pay-for-performance, for example, assume that individuals seek to be distinguished within the group, and that their colleagues approve of this happening. They also rest on the assumption that the contribution of any one member to a common task is easily distinguishable, and that no problems arise from singling him or her out for praise. None of this may, in fact, be true in more collectivist cultures.

Most of our received wisdom on this subject derives from the individualistic West, especially from theorists writing in English. The capital letter I is one of the most-used capitals in the English language. So the idea that rising individualism is a part of the rise of civilization itself needs to be treated as a cultural belief rather than a fact beyond dispute. Clearly, however, it took many centuries for the individual to emerge from the surrounding collectivity. It is generally believed that the essence of the relationship between the individual and society, at least in the West, has changed considerably since the Renaissance. In earlier societies, individuals were defined primarily in terms of their surrounding collective: the family, the clan, the tribe, the city-state, or the feudal group.

Individualism was very much to the fore during the periods of intense innovation such as the Renaissance, the Age of Exploration, the Netherlands' Golden Age, the French Enlightenment, and the industrial revolutions of Britain and America. A whole range of causes and effects have been offered to explain this.

Individualism and Religion

There is considerable evidence that individualism and collectivism follow the Protestant–Catholic religious divide. Calvinists had contracts or covenants with God and with one another for which they were personally responsible. Each Puritan worshipper approached God as a separate being, seeking justification through words. Roman Catholics have always approached God as a community of the faithful. Research has found that Catholics score higher on group choices and Protestants significantly lower. Geert Hofstede's research[2] confirms this, as do my own findings that Latin Catholic cultures, along with Asian cultures of the Pacific Rim, score lower on individualism than the Protestant West—for instance, the UK, Scandinavia (as a rule), the Netherlands, Germany, America, and Canada.

Individualism and Politics

Individualism has been adopted or opposed by different political factions in the history of countries, and the strength of that ethic today depends greatly on the fortune of its advocates. It triumphed in America, but is still strongly opposed by the French Catholic tradition. Eighteenth-century France, though, was exposed to the pleasures of individualism by Voltaire and Rousseau. Later, in the 19th century, the French socialists pointed to the positive effects of individualism, while outlining a new independence from traditional structures and rejecting the authority of religious, economic, and intellectual hierarchies. French business may have been affected forever by the fact that the pro-business French Liberal Party was in power when France fell suddenly to the Nazis in 1940. The fortunes of British individualism, at least in commerce, were affected by Mrs. Thatcher and her revolution.

DOES MODERNIZATION IMPLY INDIVIDUALISM?

That individualism, or self-orientation, is a crucial element of modern society has been argued by Ferdinand Tönnies.[3] He suggested that in modernizing we emerge from *Gemeinschaft*, a family-based, intimate social context in which the person is not sharply differentiated, into *Gesellschaft*, a workplace of individual tasks and separated responsibilities. Adam Smith, too, saw the division of labor as individualizing.[4] Max Weber saw many meanings in individualism: dignity, autonomy (meaning self-rule), privacy, and the opportunity for the person to develop.[5]

We take it for granted in many Western countries that individual geniuses create businesses, invent new products, deserve high salaries, and shape our future. But do they? How much credit is due to them, and how much is due to the patterns of organized employees? Why are Nobel Prizes for science awarded to single individuals becoming the exception? If a creative genius combines ideas, where did such ideas come from if not the community? Are we really self-made, or did our parents, teachers, families, and friends have a hand in it?

The following dilemma, which explores this dimension, shows that people from different cultures make different choices about appropriate ways of working.

There are two ways in which people can work.

A. One way is to work as an individual, alone. In this case, you are pretty much your own boss. Individuals decide most things themselves, and how they get along is their own business. You only have to take care of yourself without expecting others to look out for you.

B. Another way is working in a group where everybody works together. Everybody has something to say in the decisions that are made, and everybody can count on one another.

Which way of working do you think better represents activities in the workplace, A or B?

Figure 5–2 (page 57) shows the results of these answers. It differs from the previous illustrations of responses to dilemmas in that nationals are much more divided in their approach; the highest score choosing B is only 49 percent. However, the range between countries remains very great. Only 14 percent of Germans believe that most work is in a group such as that described in B, whereas at the other extreme this is the experience of approximately half of Czechs and Russians. This of course has a strong relationship with 1980s political organization in the latter countries.

WHICH COLLECTIVITY?

Individuals are either self- or collectivity-oriented, though we must be careful in generalizing about which collectivity a particular culture identifies with. The high internal variation of scores in my research, I believe, has to do with the numerous collectivities with which different cultures choose to identify.

Take, for example, the following question.

A defect is discovered in one of the installations. It was caused by negligence of one of the members of a team. Responsibility for this mistake can be carried in various ways.

A. The person causing the defect by negligence is the one responsible.

B. Because he or she happens to work in a team, the responsibility should be carried by the group.

Which one of these two ways of taking responsibility do you think is usually the case in your society, A or B?

FIGURE 5–2
Two Ways to Work

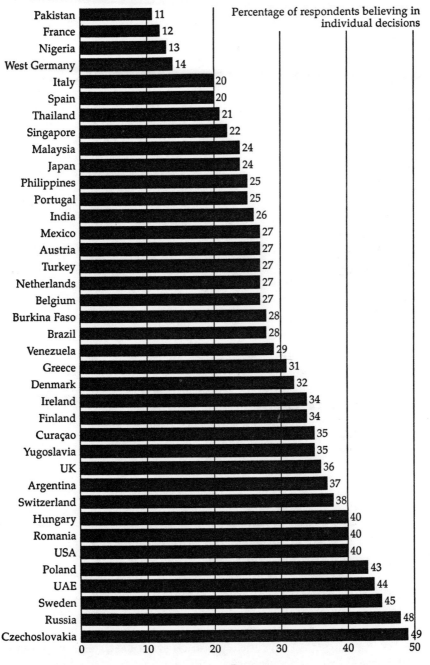

Percentage of respondents believing in individual decisions

Country	Percent
Pakistan	11
France	12
Nigeria	13
West Germany	14
Italy	20
Spain	20
Thailand	21
Singapore	22
Malaysia	24
Japan	24
Philippines	25
Portugal	25
India	26
Mexico	27
Austria	27
Turkey	27
Netherlands	27
Belgium	27
Burkina Faso	28
Brazil	28
Venezuela	29
Greece	31
Denmark	32
Ireland	34
Finland	34
Curaçao	35
Yugoslavia	35
UK	36
Argentina	37
Switzerland	38
Hungary	40
Romania	40
USA	40
Poland	43
UAE	44
Sweden	45
Russia	48
Czechoslovakia	49

Percent

This question triggers a number of scores which are consistent with the previous question, but we can also identify a number of shifts. This has to do with the heterogeneity of the concept of collectivity or group. For each single society, it is necessary to determine the group with which individuals have the closest identification. They could be keen to identify with their trade union, their family, their corporation, their religion, their profession, their nation, or the state apparatus. The French tend to identify with *la France, la famille, le cadre*; the Japanese with the corporation; the former Eastern bloc with the Communist Party; and Ireland with the Roman Catholic Church. Collective goals may be good or bad for industry depending on the collectivity concerned, its attitude, and its relevance to business development.

As Figure 5–3 (page 59) shows, the impact of communist organization on Russian and East European managers was, in this respect, extremely limited. They scored highest on the individual responsibility assumption. Americans are exactly in the middle of the range at 40 percent, rather below most European countries except the UK, which is bracketed with Japan at 36 percent individualist.

The approach to the situation will of course differ in relation to third parties. If Americans are criticized, there is a good chance that Bill will put an elbow into the stomach of Pete, while asking whose rotten idea it was, while the Italians will walk out as having suffered a group insult, regardless of the fact that it was Giorgio who did it.

IS INDIVIDUALISM A CORPORATE REQUIREMENT?

While the French experience individualism more negatively, the more optimistic philosophy of Germany sees, in the words of Simmel, "an organic unity of individual and society."[6] America, with its vast acreage available to migrating individuals, is often seen as the world's major exponent of individualism, and indeed scores highest, or nearly so, on most of our research instruments. De Tocqueville, the 19th century French aristocrat, described Americans as exhibiting "a strong confidence in self, or reliance upon one's own exertion and resources." The "Commission on National

FIGURE 5–3
Whose Fault Was It?

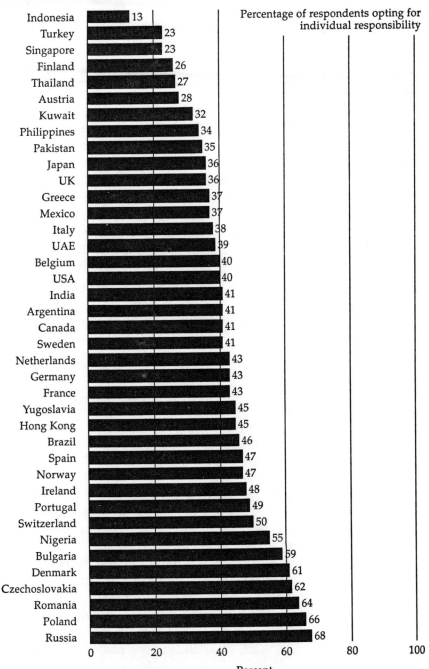

Percentage of respondents opting for individual responsibility

Country	Percent
Indonesia	13
Turkey	23
Singapore	23
Finland	26
Thailand	27
Austria	28
Kuwait	32
Philippines	34
Pakistan	35
Japan	36
UK	36
Greece	37
Mexico	37
Italy	38
UAE	39
Belgium	40
USA	40
India	41
Argentina	41
Canada	41
Sweden	41
Netherlands	43
Germany	43
France	43
Yugoslavia	45
Hong Kong	45
Brazil	46
Spain	47
Norway	47
Ireland	48
Portugal	49
Switzerland	50
Nigeria	55
Bulgaria	59
Denmark	61
Czechoslovakia	62
Romania	64
Poland	66
Russia	68

Percent

Goals," reporting to President Eisenhower, claimed that the possibility of individual self-realization was the central goal of American civilization.

Yet there are dissenting voices on the usefulness of individualism, even in America. Harvard sociologist Daniel Bell has accused consumerist-type individualism, what he terms modernism, of weakening America's industrial infrastructure.[7] As the information society develops, those with a collective ethos disseminate information faster. Information is shareable in a way physical products are not. Bell and Nelson see a shift from "tribal brotherhood" which excludes individuality, to "universal otherhood" that includes it, while still focusing upon superordinate group goals.[8]

A visionary call for the integration of individualism and collectivism came from the Emile Durkheim, the 19th century French sociologist. He saw collectivism taking both primitive and more modern forms. In its primitive form, the society has a collective conscience from which none dare deviate. The individual is dominated by the collectivity. Durkheim called this mechanical solidarity, which he saw as losing ground because industry requires a division of labor, which mechanical solidarity is slow to accommodate. This would help explain the early economic success of individualist (and Protestant) nations.

But Durkheim also saw a later, more sophisticated form of voluntary integration among sovereign beings which he called organic solidarity. The extension of the division of labor would cause the individual to share fewer and fewer characteristics with other individuals in the same society, and would call for a new form of social integration. This involved biological-type integration as found in developing organisms, which are both differentiated and integrated. In 1965, Paul Lawrence and Jay Lorsch[9] found that highly creative plastics companies, prospering in turbulent environments, were both more highly differentiated and more highly integrated. It was a vindication of the model of organic growth, and pointed to an increasingly necessary synthesis of individualism and collectivism in increasingly complex, differentiated, and interdependent societies. Charles Hampden-Turner sees the issue as essentially circular, with two "starting points" (see Figure 5–4 page 61).[10]

FIGURE 5–4
Reconciling Individualism and Collectivism

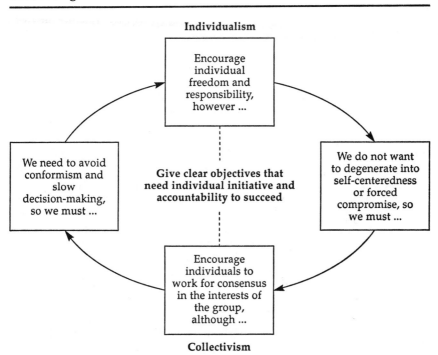

Individualism

Encourage individual freedom and responsibility, however ...

We need to avoid conformism and slow decision-making, so we must ...

Give clear objectives that need individual initiative and accountability to succeed

We do not want to degenerate into self-centeredness or forced compromise, so we must ...

Encourage individuals to work for consensus in the interests of the group, although ...

Collectivism

We all go through these cycles, but starting from different points and conceiving of them as means or ends. The individualist culture sees the individual as "the end," and improvements to collective arrangements as the means to achieve it. The collectivist culture sees the group as its end, and improvements to individual capacities as a means to that end. Yet if the relationship is truly circular, the decision to label one element as an end and another as a means is arbitrary. By definition, circles never end. Every "end" is also means to another goal.

This is closer to my own conviction that individualism finds its fulfillment in service to the group, while group goals are of demonstrable value to individuals only if those individuals are consulted and participate in the process of developing them. The reconciliation is not easy, but possible.

INDIVIDUALISM VERSUS COLLECTIVISM IN INTERNATIONAL BUSINESS

What are the practical issues raised by differences in degrees of individualism or collectivism? Consider our ongoing case of MCC and the luckless Mr. Johnson.

During a meeting in Milan, Mr. Johnson presented ideas for the payment scheme to motivate the sales force. He became annoyed at the way these meetings were always run, and decided to introduce guidelines on how all future meetings should be conducted. He did not like the Singaporean and African representatives always turning up in groups. They should, he said, confine themselves to one representative only, please. And could Mr. Sin from Singapore make sure that his boss was always represented by the same person and not different people on each occasion?

These suggestions were not very popular among some of the managers. Mr. Sin, Mr. Nuere from Nigeria, and Mr. Calamier from France wanted to know the reasons for these comments. Mr. Sin asked why, since different issues were on the agenda, they should not have different representatives knowledgeable on the various items? The discussion was going nowhere, and after an hour had passed, Mr. Johnson suggested it be put to a vote, confident that most of his European managers would back him.

But this, too, proved controversial. Mr. Calamier threw up his hands and said he was "shocked that on such a sensitive and important issue you seek to impose this decision upon a minority." He said there really should be a consensus on this even if it took another hour. Mr. Sin agreed that "voting should be saved for trivial questions."

Johnson looked to the German and Scandinavian representatives for support, but to his surprise they agreed that consensus should be given more of a chance. He was too frustrated to respond to the Dutch manager's suggestion that they should vote on whether to vote.

Finally, the Nigerians recommended that, at the very least, a discussion and/or voting should be postponed until the next meeting. How else were those present supposed to solicit the views of their colleagues in their home offices? Wearily, Mr. Johnson agreed. Further discussions about the reward system would have to wait, too.

Representation

It should be evident from this passage above that collectivist cultures prefer plural representation. The Singaporeans, Nigerians, and French seek negotiating groups, which are the microcosms of the interests of their entire national subsidiaries. In the face of unexpected demands, collectivists will wish to confer with those back home. Rarely does a single Japanese representative go to an important negotiation. Yet to Anglo-Saxons, a single representative voting on his or her private conscience on behalf of constituents is the foundation stone of parliamentary democracy. To more collectivist cultures, those at the meeting are delegates, bound by the wishes of those who sent them.

Status

Unaccompanied people in collectivist cultures are assumed to lack status. If there is no one to take notes for you or help you carry your bags, you cannot be very important. If you arrive unaccompanied in Thailand, for example, they may seriously underestimate your status and power at home.

Translators

In Anglo-Saxon negotiations, the translator is supposed to be neutral, like a black box through which words in one language enter and words in another language exit. The translator in more collectivist cultures will usually serve the national group, engaging them in lengthy asides and attempting to mediate misunderstandings arising from culture as well as language. Very often he or she may be the top negotiator in the group and is an interpreter rather than a translator.

Decision Making

Collectivist decision making typically takes much longer, and there are sustained efforts to win over everyone to achieve consensus. Voting down the dissenters, as often happens in English-speaking Western democracies, is not acceptable. There will usually be detailed consultations with all those concerned, and because of pressures to agree on collective goals, consensus will usually be achieved. If the group or home office is not consulted first, an initial "yes" can easily become a "no" later. The many minor objections raised are typically practical rather than personal or principled, and the consensus may be modified in many respects.

Since, however, those consulted will usually have to implement the consensus, this latter phase of implementation typically proceeds smoothly and easily. The time wasted (from an individualist's perspective) is saved when the new procedures operate as envisaged. The Japanese *ringi* process, where proposals circulate and are initialed by agreeing participants, is the most famous example of collectivist decision making, but it can lead to very lengthy delays.

A Japanese company had a factory built in the south of the Netherlands. As usual, this was carried out with acute attention to detail. In the designing phase, though, it discovered that it had not considered one restriction. The legal minimum height for workshops was 4cm higher than the design. A new design, which needed extensive consultation with many people at the head office in Tokyo, took one full month per centimeter for approval.

But it is far too easy for North Americans and Northwest Europeans, used to individualism, to jeer at such delays. Our own procedures can err in the opposite direction. The decision-making process in individualistic cultures is usually very short, with a "lonely individualist" making "deathless decisions" in a few fateful seconds. While this may make for quicker deliberations, one-minute managers, and so on, it will often be discovered months later that the organization has conspired to defeat decisions managers never liked or agreed to. Saving time in decision making is often followed by significant delays due to implementation problems.

The individualist society, with its respect for individual opinions, will frequently ask for a vote to get all noses pointing in the same direction. The drawback to this is that within a short time they are likely to have reverted to their original orientation. The collectivist society will intuitively refrain from voting because this will not show respect to the individuals who are against the majority decision. It prefers to deliberate until consensus is reached. The final result takes longer to achieve, but will be much more stable. In individualistic societies, there is frequently disparity between decision and implementation.

INDIVIDUALISM, COLLECTIVISM, AND MOTIVATION

The relationship between individual and group also plays an important role in what motivates people. Mr. Johnson believed that he and MCC knew what motivated people: extra salary rewards paid to high-performing individuals. It had seemed so obvious in the meetings back in Missouri, but now he was having doubts. After the earlier discussion, could he be sure of anything?

Mr. Johnson finally managed to compromise on the representation issue by allowing each national office to send up to three people, if they wished, but no more. This decision had not been voted on. Everyone had agreed. Now he could start to tackle the introduction of pay-for-performance, bonuses, and merit pay for next year.

He started, as usual, with an overview of the situation in America. It had been three years since the system was first introduced. In general, he explained, they could detect a link between the use of this system and computer sales, although it had to be mentioned that a similar system had failed miserably in the manufacturing department. A different type of achievement-based reward system was currently being tested. No problems were anticipated with this revised system. "In summary," Johnson said, "we are strongly convinced that we need to introduce this system worldwide."

The Northwest European representatives voiced their carefully considered, but positive, comments. Then the Italian representative, Mr. Gialli, began describing his experience with the system. In his country, the pay-for-performance experiment did much better than he had expected during the first three months. But the following three months were disastrous. Sales were dramatically lower for the salesperson who had performed the best during the previous period. "After many discussions," he continued, "I finally discovered what was happening. The salesperson who received the bonus for the previous period felt guilty in front of the others, and tried extremely hard the next quarter not to earn a bonus."

The Italian manager concluded that, for the next year of this experiment, the Italian market should be divided into nine regions. All sales representatives within one region should be allowed to allocate the bonus earned in their region either to individual performers or to share it equally. The blunt Dutch manager's reaction was: "I have never heard such a crazy idea."

This incident shows that there are at least two sources of motivation. People work for extrinsic money rewards and for the positive regard and support of their colleagues. In more collectivist cultures, this second source of motivation may be so strong that high performers prefer to share the fruits of their efforts with colleagues than to take extra money for themselves as individuals.

Western theories of motivation have individuals growing out of early, and hence primitive, social needs into an individually resplendent self-actualization at the summit of the hierarchy. Needless to say, this does not achieve resonance the world over, however good a theory it may be for America and Northwest Europe. The Japanese notion of the highest good is harmonious relationships within and with the patterns of nature; the primary orientation is to other people and to the natural world.

DIFFERENCES IN ORGANIZATIONAL STRUCTURE

In individualistic cultures, organizations (from the Greek *organon*) are essentially instruments. They have been deliberately assembled and contrived in order to serve individual owners, employees, and customers. Members of organizations enter relationships because it is in their individual interests to do so. Their ties are abstract, legal ones, regulated by contract.

The organization is a means to what its actors want for themselves. Insofar as they cooperate, it is because they have particular interests at stake. Each performs a differentiated and specialized function and receives an extrinsic reward for doing so. Authority originates in an individual's skill at performing tasks, and an individual's knowledge is used to make the organizational instrument work effectively.

In collective cultures, the organization is not the creation or the instrument of its founders so much as a social context all members share and which gives them meaning and purpose. Organizations are often likened to a large family, community, or clan which develops and nurtures its members and may live longer than they do. The growth and prosperity of organizations are not considered bonanzas for individual shareholders or gravy trains for top managers, but are valuable ends in themselves. These considerations will be discussed in depth in Chapter 11.

PRACTICAL TIPS FOR DOING BUSINESS IN INDIVIDUALIST AND COLLECTIVIST CULTURES

Recognizing the Differences

Individualism	Collectivism
1. More frequent use of "I" form.	1. More frequent use of "We" form.

2. Decisions made on the spot by representatives.
3. People ideally achieve alone and assume personal responsibility.
4. Vacations taken in pairs, or even alone.

2. Decisions referred back by delegate to organization.
3. People ideally achieve in groups which assume joint responsibility.
4. Vacations in organized groups or with extended family.

Tips for Doing Business with:

Individualists (for collectivists)	Collectivists (for individualists)
1. Prepare for quick decisions and sudden offers not referred to HQ.	1. Show patience for time taken to consent and to consult.
2. Negotiator can commit those who sent him or her and is very reluctant to go back on an undertaking.	2. Negotiator can only agree tentatively and may withdraw an undertaking after consulting with superiors.
3. The toughest negotiations were probably already done within the organization while preparing for the meeting. You have a tough job selling them the solution to this meeting.	3. The toughest negotiations are with the collectivists you face. You must somehow persuade them to cede to you points which the multiple interests in your company demand.
4. Conducting business alone means that this person is respected by his or her company and has its esteem.	4. Conducting business when surrounded by helpers means that this person has high status in his or her company.
5. The aim is to make a quick deal.	5. The aim is to build lasting relationships.

When Managing and Being Managed

Individualists	Collectivists
1. Try to adjust individual needs to organizational needs.	1. Seek to integrate personality with authority within the group.
2. Introduce methods of individual incentives like pay-for-performance, individual assessment, MBO.	2. Give attention to esprit de corps, morale, and cohesiveness.
3. Expect job turnover and mobility to be high.	3. Have lower job turnover and mobility.
4. Seek out high performers, heroes, and champions for special praise.	4. Extol the whole group and avoid showing favoritism.
5. Give people the freedom to take individual initiatives.	5. Hold up superordinate goals for all to meet.

REFERENCES

1. Parsons, T., and E. A. Shils, *Towards a General Theory of Action*, Harvard University Press, Cambridge, Mass., 1951.
2. Hofstede, G. *Culture's Consequences*, Sage, London, 1980.
3. Tönnies, F., *Community and Society* (trans. C. P. Loomis), Harper & Row, New York, 1957.
4. Smith, A., *The Wealth of Nations*.
5. Weber, M., *The Theory of Social and Economic Organization*, Free Press, New York, 1947.
6. Simmel, G., *The Sociology of Simmel* (trans. K. H. Wolff), Scott, Foresman, Glenview, Illinois, 1950.
7. Bell, D., *The Cultural Contradictions of Capitalism*, Basic Books, New York, 1976.
8. Bell, D. and B. Nelson, *The Idea of Usury*, University of Chicago Press, Chicago, 1969.
9. Lawrence, P. R., and J. W. Lorsch, *Organization and Environment: Managing Differentiation and Integration*, Irwin, Homewood, Illinois, 1967.
10. Hampden-Turner, C., *Charting the Corporate Mind*, Basil Blackwell, 1991. Adapted with the permission of The Free Press, a Division of Macmillan, Inc. from *Charting the Corporate Mind:* Graphic Solutions to Business Conflicts by Charles Hampden-Turner. Copyright © 1990 by The Free Press.

Chapter Six

Feelings and Relationships

In relationships between people, reason and emotion both play a role. Which of these dominates will depend upon whether we are **affective** (that is, we show our emotions), in which case we probably get an emotional response in return, or whether we are emotionally **neutral** in our approach.

AFFECTIVE VERSUS NEUTRAL CULTURES

Members of cultures which are affectively neutral do not telegraph their feelings, but keep them carefully controlled and subdued. In contrast, in cultures high on affectivity, people show their feelings plainly by laughing, smiling, grimacing, scowling, and gesturing; they attempt to find immediate outlets for their feelings.

We should be careful not to over-interpret such differences. Neutral cultures are not necessarily cold or unfeeling, nor are they emotionally constipated or repressed. The amount of emotion we show is often the result of convention. In a culture in which feelings are controlled, irrepressible joy or grief will still signal loudly. In a culture where feelings are amplified, they will have to be signaled more loudly still in order to register at all. In cultures where everyone emotes, we may not find words or expressions adequate for our strongest feelings, since they have all been used up.

A workshop exercise under this heading asks participants how they would behave if they felt upset about something at work. Would they express their feelings openly? Figure 6–1 shows the relative positions of 10 countries on the extent to which exhibiting emotion is acceptable. It is least acceptable in Japan, where our database shows a score of 83 percent on the neutral orientation. There are considerable variances between European countries, with West

FIGURE 6–1
Feeling Upset at Work

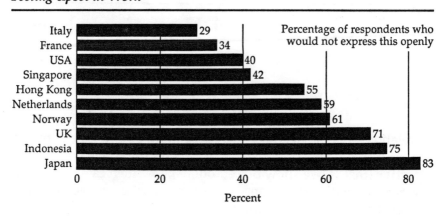

Germany the most neutral (75 percent) and Italy and France the least (29 percent and 34 percent respectively). Note that Hong Kong and Singapore both score much lower than Japan and Indonesia; there is no general pattern by continent.

Typically, reason and emotion are of course combined. In expressing ourselves, we try to find confirmation of our thoughts and feelings in the response of our audience. When our own approach is highly emotional, we are seeking a **direct** emotional response: "I have the same feelings as you on this subject." When our own approach is highly neutral, we are seeking an **indirect** response. "Because I agree with your reasoning or proposition, I give you my support."

On both occasions, approval is being sought, but different paths are being used to this end. The indirect path gives us emotional support contingent upon the success of an effort of intellect. The direct path allows our feelings about a factual proposition to show through, thereby joining feelings with thoughts in a different way.

Consider a scene in which the Italian office of MCC has made a proposal to allow the sales personnel to decide as a group whether they wish to have individual incentives or to share bonus payments among the whole team, while identifying the persons responsible for winning the bonus. You will recall that this was the idea Mr. Bergman, the Dutch representative, called "crazy" in Chapter 5.

Raising his voice, Mr. Pauli, Gialli's colleague, asked: "What do you mean, a crazy idea? We have carefully considered the pros and cons, and consider that it would greatly benefit the buyer."

"Please, don't get overexcited," pleaded Mr. Johnson. "We need to provide solid arguments, and should not get sidetracked by emotional irrelevancies."

Before Bergman had a chance to explain why he thought it was a crazy idea, the two Italian colleagues left the room for a time-out. "This is what I call a typical Italian reaction," Mr. Bergman remarked to his colleagues. "Before I even had a chance to give my arguments as to why I think the idea is crazy, they walk out."

The other managers were squirming uncomfortably in their chairs. They did not know what to think. Mr. Johnson got up and left the room to talk to the Italians.

It is easy for the British, North Americans, or Northwest Europeans to sympathize with Johnson or Bergman about "excitable" Italians. After all, the incentive system either works or it does not. This will not change, however strongly we feel. It is a matter of trial and observation. According to this approach, neutrality is a means to an end. The time to get emotional is when the incentives work or fail to work, at which point pleasure or disappointment are appropriate. After all, control of our feelings is a sign of civilization, is it not?

Such explanations show that we can adduce good reasons for any cultural norm. The Italians were angry because they identified emotionally with their sales team and knew intuitively that working hard for each other as well as for customers was the motivation of an excellent salesperson. They felt they knew how their sales force would feel about the emotional rewards for hard work. Mr. Bergman's "reasonable judgment" was not relevant to the Italians. Since when is the intrinsic pleasure found in work a matter of "fact" anyway? It is deeply personal and cultural. As Pascal wrote: "The heart has its reasons which reason knows not of." But he was a Frenchman.

DEGREES OF AFFECTIVITY IN DIFFERENT CULTURES

The amount of visible emoting is a major difference between cultures. We may think that a Frenchman who curses us in a traffic accident is truly enraged, close to committing violence. In fact, he may simply be getting his view of the facts in first, and may expect an equal stream of vituperation from us in return. He may, indeed, be further from violence as a result of this expression. There are norms about acceptable levels of vehemence, and these can be much higher in some countries than in others.

Americans, for example, tend to be on the expressive side. Perhaps this is because, with so many immigrants and such a large country, they have had to break down social barriers again and again. The habit of using diminutives (Chuck instead of Charles, Bob instead of Robert), "smile" buttons, welcome wagons, and the speed with which cordial and informal relationships are made, all testify to the need to resocialize in new neighborhoods several times in a lifetime.

This is a very different experience from life in smaller countries like Sweden, the Netherlands, Denmark, Norway, and so on. There it may be harder to avoid than to meet those of your generation with whom you grew up. Friendships tend to start early in life and last many years, so the need to be effusive with relative strangers is much less.

The Control or Release of Emotion

There is a tendency for those with norms of emotional neutrality to dismiss anger, delight, or intensity in the workplace as unprofessional. Mr. Pauli at MCC has obviously "lost his cool," a judgment which assumes the desirability of a cool exterior to begin with. In fact, Pauli probably regards Bergman as emotionally dead, or as hiding his true feelings behind a mask of deceit. As we shall see in Chapter 7 when we go on to discuss how specific, as opposed to diffuse, emotions can be, there are really two issues wrapped up in the question of emotional display. Should emotion be **exhibited** in business relations? Should it be **separated** from reasoning processes lest it corrupt them?

Americans tend to exhibit emotion, yet separate it from objective and rational decisions. Italians and South European nations in general tend to **exhibit and not separate**. Dutch and Swedes tend **not to exhibit and to separate**. Once again, there is nothing "good" or "bad" about these differences. You can argue that emotions held in check will twist your judgments despite all efforts to be rational. Or you can argue that pouring forth emotions makes it harder for anyone present to think straight. Similarly, you can scoff at the walls separating reasons from emotions, or argue that because of the leakage that so often occurs, these should be thicker and stronger.

North Europeans watching a South European politician on television disapprove of waving hands and other gestures. So do the Japanese, whose saying, "Only a dead fish has an open mouth," compares with the English, "Empty vessels make the most noise."

Beware Humor, Understatement, or Irony

Cultures also vary on the permissible use of humor. In Britain or America, we often start our workshops with a cartoon or anecdote which makes a joke about the main points to be covered. This is always a success. But when one of the first workshops in Germany was launched, with some confidence, with a cartoon deriding European cultural differences, nobody laughed. Indeed, the audience looked aggressive. As the week went by, however, there was a lot of laughter in the bar, and eventually even in the sessions. It was simply not permissible, in a professional setting, between strangers.

The British use humor a lot to release emotions dammed up behind the stiff upper lip. They also regard understatement as funny. If a Briton speaks of being "underwhelmed" by someone's presentation, or of regarding it with "modified rapture," that is a way of **controlling** emotional expression, while at the same time triggering emotional release in the form of laughter. The individual thereby has it both ways. A Japanese superior will similarly rebuke an incompetent subordinate by exaggerated deference. "If you could see your way to kindly troubling yourself in a matter so minor, I would be in your debt." In affective language, this translates as "Do it or else."

Unfortunately, understatements of this kind, along with throwaway lines and jokes, are almost always lost on foreigners, even if they speak the language well enough for normal discourse. Humor is language-dependent and relies on a very quick sense of the meaning of words. The statement, "She was a good cook, as cooks go, and as cooks go she went," is only funny if you are familiar with the colloquialism "as (something) goes," meaning "compared with other (somethings)," in which case "went" takes you by surprise.

Not only is it hard for foreigners to release emotion in this way, but they are unlikely to grasp that understatements are actually intended ironically. They are more likely to see the English or Japanese as being opaque, as usual. Any statement which means the opposite to what it literally states may be hard on foreign managers, and should be avoided. If insiders all laugh, the foreigner feels excluded, deprived of the emotional release the rest have enjoyed.

INTERCULTURAL COMMUNICATION

There are a variety of problems of communication across cultural boundaries which arise from the differences between affective and neutral approaches. In our workshops, we frequently ask the participants to describe the concept of intercultural communication. They list instruments—language, body language—and more general definitions like the exchange of messages and ideas. Communication is, of course, essentially the **exchange of information,** be it words, ideas, or emotions. Information, in turn, is the **carrier of meaning.** Communication is only possible between people who to some extent share a system of meaning, so here we return to our basic definition of culture.

Verbal Communication

Western society has a predominately verbal culture. We communicate with paper, film, and conversation. Two of the best-selling computer programs in the Western world, word processing and graphics, have been developed to support verbal communication. We become nervous and uneasy once we stop talking. But we have very different styles of discussion. For the Anglo-Saxon, when A stops, B starts. It is not polite to interrupt. The even more verbal Latins integrate slightly more than this; B will frequently interrupt A and vice versa to show how interested each is in what the other is saying.

The pattern of silent communication shown in Figure 6–2 for oriental languages frightens the westerner. The moment of silence is interpreted as a failure to communicate. But this is a misunderstanding. Let us reverse the roles; how can the westerner commu-

FIGURE 6–2
Styles of Verbal Communication

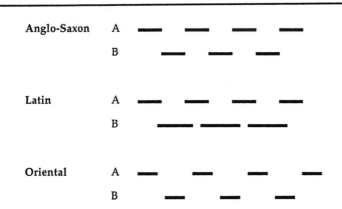

nicate clearly if the other person is not given time to finish his or her sentence, or to digest what the other has been saying? It is a sign of respect for the other person if you take time to process the information without talking yourself.

Tone of voice. Another cross-cultural problem arises from tone of voice. Figure 6–3 (page 76) shows typical patterns for Anglo-Saxon, Latin, and oriental languages. For some neutral societies, ups and downs in speech suggest that the speaker is not serious. But in most Latin societies, this exaggerated way of communicating shows that you have your heart in the matter. Oriental societies tend to have a much more monotonous style; self-controlled, it shows respect. Frequently, the higher the position a person holds, the lower and flatter the voice.

A British manager posted to Nigeria found that it was very effective to raise his voice for important issues. His Nigerian subordinates saw this unexpected explosion by a normally self-controlled manager as a sign of extra concern. After success in Nigeria, he was posted to Malaysia. Shouting there was a sign of loss of face; his colleagues did not take him seriously, and he was transferred.

The spoken word. The most obvious verbal process is the spoken word. Regardless of rhythm, pace, or humor, this needs to

FIGURE 6–3
Tone of Voice

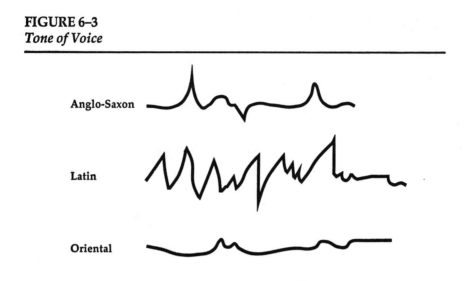

Anglo-Saxon

Latin

Oriental

be taken into consideration. The English-speaking nations have the enormous advantage of more than 300 million speakers who understand their language. However, as we all know, even the English and Americans are seperated by a common language which is used quite differently in different contexts, and which has some serious differences in the meanings of individual words. English speakers also face an enormous disadvantage, which is that it is very difficult ever to speak another language; its nationals will only allow you so much accent before switching to English themselves. To express yourself in another language is a necessary, if not a sufficient, condition for understanding another culture.

Nonverbal Communication

Research has shown that at least 75 percent of all communication is nonverbal. This figure is the minimum for the most verbal cultures of all. In western societies, **eye contact** is crucial to confirm interest. However, the amount differs sharply from society to society. An Italian visiting professor at Wharton arrived on campus and was surprised to be greeted by a number of students. His expressive Italian nature drove him eventually to catch one of them and ask him if he knew who he was. The student said he was afraid he did not. "So why did you greet me?" "Because it seemed like you knew me, sir." The professor realized that, in America, eye contact between strangers is only supposed to last for a split second.

Leonel Brug, a colleague at the Centre for International Business Studies, was brought up in both Curaçao and Suriname. As a boy he would try to avoid eye contact, whereupon his Curaçao grandmother would slap him in the face (in some cultures body talk is very effective) and say, "Look me in the face." Respecting an elder involves eye contact. Leonel learned fast, and when in Suriname looked his other grandmother straight in the face to show respect. She slapped him, too; respectful kids in Suriname do not make eye contact.

Touching other people, the **space** it is normal to keep between you, and assumptions about **privacy** are all further manifestations of affective or neutral cultures. Never help an Arab lady out of a bus; it might cost you your contract.

RECONCILING NEUTRAL AND AFFECTIVE CULTURES

Overly neutral or affective (expressive) cultures have problems in doing business with each other. The neutral person is easily accused of being icecold with no heart; the affective person is seen as out of control and inconsistent. When such cultures meet, the first essential is to recognize the differences, and to refrain from making any judgments based on emotions, or the lack of them.

PRACTICAL TIPS FOR DOING BUSINESS IN NEUTRAL AND AFFECTIVE CULTURES

Recognizing the Differences

Neutral	*Affective*
1. Do not reveal what they are thinking or feeling.	1. Reveal thoughts and feelings verbally and nonverbally.
2. May (accidentally) reveal tension in face and posture.	2. Transparency and expressiveness release tensions.
3. Emotions often dammed up; will occasionally explode.	3. Emotions flow easily, effusively, vehemently, and without inhibition.

Recognizing the Differences (concluded)

Neutral	Affective
4. Cool and self-possessed conduct is admired.	4. Heated, vital, animated expressions admired.
5. Physical contact, gesturing, or strong facial expressions often taboo.	5. Touching, gesturing, and strong facial expressions common.
6. Statements often read out in monotone.	6. Statements declaimed fluently and dramatically.

Tips for Doing Business with:

Neutrals (for affectives)	Affectives (for neutrals)
1. Ask for time-outs from meetings and negotiations where you can patch each other up and rest between games of poker with the Impassive Ones.	1. Do not be put off your stride when they create scenes and get histrionic; take time-outs for sober reflection and hard assessments.
2. Put as much as you can on paper beforehand.	2. When they are expressing goodwill, respond warmly.
3. Their lack of emotional tone does not mean they are disinterested or bored, only that they do not like to show their hand.	3. Their enthusiasm, readiness to agree, or vehement disagreement does not mean that they have made up their minds.
4. The entire negotiation is typically focused on the object or proposition being discussed, not so much on you as persons.	4. The entire negotiation is typically focused on you as persons, not so much on the object or proposition being discussed.

When Managing and Being Managed

Neutrals	Affectives
1. Avoid warm, expressive, or enthusiastic behaviors. These are interpreted as lack of control over your feelings and inconsistent with high status.	1. Avoid detached, ambiguous, and cool demeanor. This will be interpreted as negative evaluation, as disdain, dislike, and social distance. You are excluding them from "the family."
2. If you prepare extensively beforehand, you will find it easier to stick to the point, that is, the neutral topics being discussed.	2. If you discover whose work, energy, and enthusiasm has been invested in which projects, you are more likely to appreciate tenacious positions.
3. Look for small cues that the person is pleased or angry, and amplify their importance.	3. Tolerate great surfeits of emotionality without getting intimidated or coerced, and moderate their importance.

Chapter Seven

How Far We Get Involved

Closely related to whether we show emotions in dealing with other people is the degree to which we engage others in **specific** areas of life and single levels of personality, or **diffusely** in multiple areas of our lives and at several levels of personality at the same time.

SPECIFIC VERSUS DIFFUSE CULTURES

In specific-oriented cultures, a manager **segregates out** the task relationship she or he has with a subordinate and insulates this from other dealings. Say a manager supervises the sale of integrated circuits. Were he to meet one of his sales reps in the bar, on the golf course, on vacation, or in the local superstore, almost none of his authority would diffuse itself into these relationships. Indeed, he might defer to the sales rep as a more skilled shopper, or ask advice on improving his golf game. Each area in which the two encounter each other is considered apart from the other, a **specific** case.

However, in some countries, every life space and every level of personality tends to permeate all others. *Monsieur le directeur* is a formidable authority wherever you encounter him. If he runs the company, it is generally expected that his opinions on *haute cuisine* are better than those of his subordinates. His taste in clothes and value as a citizen are all permeated by his directorship, and he probably expects to be deferred to by those who know him, whether in the street, the club, or a shop. Of course, reputation always leaks to some extent into other areas of life. This extent is what we measure for specificity (small) versus diffuseness (large).

Kurt Lewin,[1] the German-American psychologist, represented the personality as a series of concentric circles with "life spaces" or "personality levels" between. The most personal and private spaces are near the center. The most shared and public spaces are at the outer peripheries. As a German-Jewish refugee in America, Lewin was able to contrast U-type (American) life spaces with G-type (German) life spaces.These are illustrated in Figure 7–1.

Lewin's circles show Americans, in the U-type circle, as having much more public than private space, segregated into many specific sections. The American citizen can have a standing and reputation at work, in the bowling league, at the Parent–Teachers' Association, at the Oddfellows Hall, among fellow computer hackers, and in the local chapter of the Veterans of Foreign Wars. Colleagues who enter any of these spaces are not necessarily close or lifetime buddies. They may not feel free to call on you if the subject is not computers or bowling. One reason why the American personality is so friendly and accessible (illustrated by the dotted lines) is that being admitted into one public layer is not a very big commitment. You "know" the other person for limited purposes only.

Contrast this with the G-type circle. Here, access to life spaces is guarded by a thick line. It is hard to enter, and you need the other's permission. The public space is relatively small. The private spaces are large and **diffuse,** which means that, once a friend is admitted, this lets him or her into all, or nearly all, your private spaces. Moreover, your standing and reputation cross over these spaces.

Herr Doktor Muller is Herr Doktor Muller at his university, at the butcher's, and at the garage; his wife is also Frau Doktor Muller in the market, at the local school, and wherever she goes. She is not simply joined diffusely to her husband, but to his job and title. In America, in contrast, I have been introduced at a reception following a graduation ceremony as Dr. Trompenaars, but at a party for much the same people a few hours later as Fons Trompenaars. I have also been introduced as "I want you all to meet my very good friend Fons . . . (what's your surname?)." In America, a title is a **specific** label for a **specific** job in a **specific** place.

For all these reasons, Germans may be thought of by Americans as remote and hard to get to know. Americans may be thought of by Germans as cheerful, garrulous, yet superficial people who let you into a very small corner of their public lives and regard you as peripheral.

Borders and barriers between "life spaces" have physical dimensions as well. I remember arriving as a student at the Wharton

FIGURE 7–1
Lewin's Circles (Author's Adaptation)

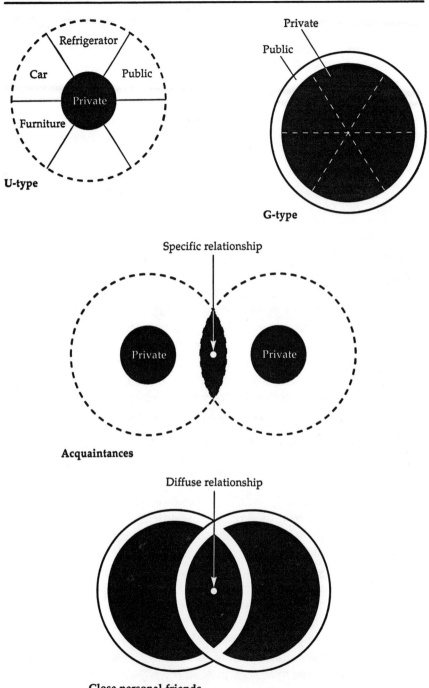

U-type

G-type

Specific relationship

Acquaintances

Diffuse relationship

Close personal friends

School in Philadelphia, Pennsylvania. Bill, a new American friend, rushed to help me move in. In gratitude for his hard work on the hot summer day, I asked him to stay for a while and have a beer. I went to wash up and came back to get him a beer out of the refrigerator. I did not need to; he had already opened the refrigerator and was helping himself. For him, a refrigerator was my public space into which I had invited him. To me and most of my Dutch compatriots, it was definitely private space.

A few days later, I was struck by a similar event. I was inquiring about transportation across town when Denise, a fellow student, tossed me her car keys and told me to call her when I was finished with my errand. I could not believe it. To me, a car was certainly private space. Have you ever tried to borrow a German acquaintance's Mercedes?

In America, where people are relatively mobile, furniture, cars, and so on, can be semi-public. People moving will hold garage sales, exhibiting very personal items on tables in a yard for all not only to see, but to purchase. They may be as open with intimate personal experiences. It is not rare to be regaled at a cocktail party with confessions of sexual incompatibility from a complete stranger. You even suspect he has forgotten your name by the time his adventure concludes. An American cartoon by Jules Feiffer[2] has the anti-hero, Bernard Mergendeiler, explain to his audience:

> I met this **marvelous** girl. I've told all my friends and colleagues at work. I go up to strangers in the street and tell them about her. I've told nearly **everyone**—except her. Why give her the advantage?

Clearly this character's public spaces overwhelm his private one. He confesses in the first to avoid communication in the second.

The situation in France or Germany is quite different. You have only to note the high hedges and shuttered windows to appreciate French concern for large private spaces. If you are invited to dinner in a French home, that invitation extends to the rooms in which that hospitality occurs. If you start wandering around the house, you may offend. If your hostess goes into her study to find a book you are discussing, and you follow her, that may be considered a trespass into her private domain. The concentric circles are not simply in the mind, but refer to spaces in which we live.

The concepts of the specific and the diffuse help us to make sense of the dispute being described in the MCC head office, which involved Mr. Johnson (American), Mr. Bergman (Dutch) and Messrs. Gialli and Pauli (Italian). Both Mr. Johnson and Mr. Bergman, while not in agreement on permissible levels of emotional expression (Mr. Johnson being more affective), **are** in agreement on the separation of reason from emotion. Americans and Dutch both believe that there are specific times, places, and spaces for being reasonable, and specific times, places, and spaces for being affective. To their perplexity and dismay, the Italians have thrown a tantrum in the middle of a meeting on serious, professional issues.

Let us continue the story.

As the representative from the head office, Mr. Johnson felt very responsible for the developments at the meeting. The Italians' behavior seemed strange to him. Mr. Bergman just wanted to discuss an important aspect of the consistency of the reward system, and they did not even give him a chance to explain his position. Moreover, the Italians had refused to put any solid arguments on the table themselves.

When Johnson entered Mr. Gialli's room, he said: "Paolo, what's the problem? You shouldn't take this too seriously. It's just a business discussion."

"Just a business discussion?" Gialli asked with unconcealed rage. "This has nothing to do with a business discussion. It is typical for that Dutchman to attack us. We have our own ways of being effective, and then he calls us crazy."

"I didn't hear that," Johnson said. "He simply said that he found your group bonus idea crazy. I know Bergman, and he didn't intend that to refer to you."

"If that's so," answered Gialli, "why is he behaving so rudely?"

Johnson realized how deeply his Italian colleagues had been offended. He went back to Bergman, took him aside, and told him about his conversation with Gialli. "Offended!" said Bergman. "Let them have the self-control to respond to professional arguments. I don't understand why they are so hot-headed anyway. They know we have done extensive research on this. Let them listen first. You have to remember that these Latins never want to be bothered with facts."

The Italian reaction is, of course, quite understandable if we grasp that their feelings about group bonuses as opposed to individual bonuses, their sympathy with their sales force and customers, and the proposal they put forward are **one diffuse whole**. To call the idea crazy is to call **them** crazy and to question their ability to represent the cultural views of fellow Italians. It offends them deeply. Their ideas are not separated from themselves. If they

FIGURE 7–2
The Danger Zone: The Specific–Diffuse Encounter

Danger Zone

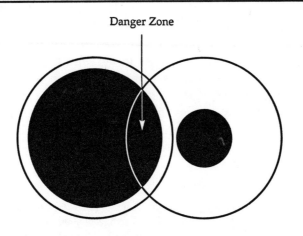

thought of it and if it represents Italian thinking, then the proposition is an extension of their personal honor.

One problem with the overlap between U-types and G-types is that the U-type sees as impersonal something the G-type sees as highly personal. Italian views on the effectiveness of group bonuses are tied to their diffuse sense of private space. It is not "just a business discussion" taking place in a realm apart from their private selves, but a discussion touching on what it means to be a feeling, thinking Italian. Pleasure and pain, acceptance and rejection ramify more widely in the diffuse system. You cannot criticize Italians as "generators of a crazy idea" without profoundly affecting their whole system.

When Americans "let in" a German, French, or Italian colleague into one compartment of their public space and show their customary openness and friendliness, that person may assume that they have been admitted to diffuse private space. They may expect the American to show equivalent friendship in all life spaces and be offended if he or she comes to their town without contacting them. They may also be offended by criticism on a professional level, which they take to be an attack by a close friend. Or they may be offended when admiration between electronic engineers goes no deeper than that.

Losing Face

Specific cultures, with their small areas of privacy clearly separated from public life, have considerable freedom for direct speech. "Do not take this personally" is a frequent observation. In relationships with diffuse people, this approach can be an insult.

American and Dutch managers find it particularly easy to insult their opposite diffuse partners (see Mr. Johnson's problems with the Italians, above). This is because they do not understand the principle of losing face, which is what happens when something is made public which people perceive as being private. The importance of avoiding loss of face is why, in diffuse cultures, so much more time is taken to get to the point; it is necessary to avoid private confrontation because it is impossible for participants not to take things personally.

I try to avoid asking a Dutch audience for criticism after one of my workshops; the experience is much the same as being machine-gunned. Afterwards, however, they tend to ask the corpse for the next date it will be available. In contrast, English and French managers will make a few mild suggestions in a context of positive congratulations, never to be heard from again.

At an international university at which I was teaching, a Ghanaian student wrote a paper for me which I was unable to grade at more than four out of ten, a fail. All scores were posted on a bulletin board. The student said that this would be a public insult to him, impossible for me as a respected professor to perpetrate, although he agreed with the mark. What I should do was to mark the paper "I" (incomplete) for the board, while feeding the actual grade into the system.

National Differences

National differences are sharp under the headings of specificity and diffuseness. The range is illustrated well by responses to the following situation.

> A boss asks a subordinate to help him paint his house. The subordinate, who does not feel like doing it, discusses the situation with a colleague.
>
> **A.** The colleague argues: "You don't have to paint if you don't feel like it. He is your boss at work. Outside, he has little authority."

B. The subordinate argues: "Despite the fact that I don't feel like it,
I will paint it. He is my boss and you can't ignore that outside of
work either."

In specific societies, where work and private life are sharply separated, managers are not at all inclined to assist. As one Dutch re-
spondent observed: "House painting is not in my collective labor
agreement." Figure 7–3 shows the proportion of managers that
would not paint the house, around 90 percent or higher in the UK,
America, Australia, and most of Northern Europe. In Japan 83 percent would not either, but in the diffuse Asian societies of China,
Nepal, and Indonesia the majority would. (Surprised by the Japanese score, we reinterviewed some Japanese respondents. They
replied that it most probably had to do with the fact that the Japanese never paint houses, which illustrates the relativity of empirical
data.) The range of differences is not so steeply graded as when
we looked at the basic cultural divides of Chapters 3 and 4, but it is
nevertheless clearly a source of deep potential incomprehension.

NEGOTIATING THE SPECIFIC–DIFFUSE CULTURAL DIVIDE

Doing business with a culture more diffuse than our own feels very
time-consuming. Some nations refuse to do business in a mental
subdivision called "commerce" or "work" which is kept apart from
the rest of life. In diffuse cultures, everything is connected to everything. Your business partner may wish to know where you went
to school, who your friends are, what you think of life, politics, art,
literature, and music. This is not a waste of time because such preferences reveal character and form friendships. They also make de-
ception nearly impossible.

As with the example in Chapter 1 of the Swedish company
(which beat an American company with a technically superior
product for a contract with an Argentinian customer), the upfront
investment in building relationships in such cultures is as important as, if not more important than, the deal. The Swedes invested a
whole week in the selling trip, the first five days of which were not
related to the business at all. They just shared the diffuse life spaces
of their hosts, talking about common interests. Only **after** a "private

FIGURE 7–3
House Painting

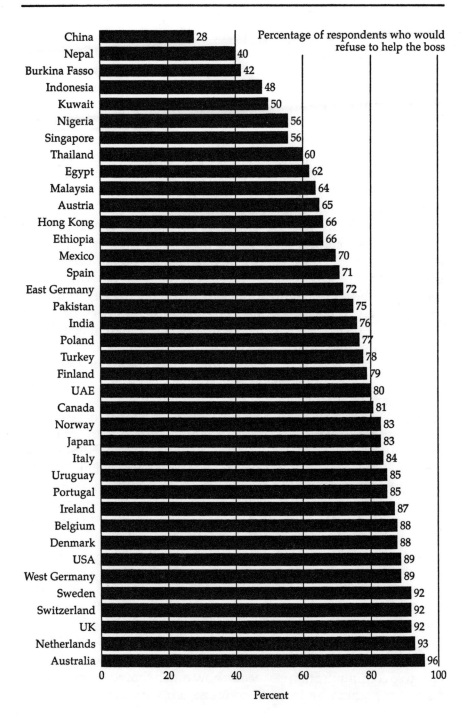

Percentage of respondents who would refuse to help the boss

Country	Percent
China	28
Nepal	40
Burkina Fasso	42
Indonesia	48
Kuwait	50
Nigeria	56
Singapore	56
Thailand	60
Egypt	62
Malaysia	64
Austria	65
Hong Kong	66
Ethiopia	66
Mexico	70
Spain	71
East Germany	72
Pakistan	75
India	76
Poland	77
Turkey	78
Finland	79
UAE	80
Canada	81
Norway	83
Japan	83
Italy	84
Uruguay	85
Portugal	85
Ireland	87
Belgium	88
Denmark	88
USA	89
West Germany	89
Sweden	92
Switzerland	92
UK	92
Netherlands	93
Australia	96

Percent

space" relationship had been established were the Argentinians willing to talk business. And that had to include several life spaces, not just one. In contrast, the Americans invested only two days in the trip, knowing they had a superior product and presentation, and were turned down.

It is really a question of priority. Do you start with the specific and neutral proposition and later get to know those interested in that proposition? Or do you start with people you can trust because you invited them into multiple life spaces, and then move on to business? Both approaches make good sense to those living in that culture, but each plays havoc with the other.

The American team found themselves continually interrupted by personal questions and social distractions, and when the corporate jet arrived on schedule to take them home, they had not adequately covered the business agenda. The Argentinians, to the Americans, seemed unable or unwilling to stick to the point. The Argentinians, for their part, found the Americans too direct, impersonal, and pushy. They were surprised by the Americans' apparent belief that you could use logic to force someone to agree with you.

In other words, specificity and diffuseness are about strategies for getting to know other people.

The diagram on the left of Figure 7–4 shows the typically diffuse strategy common in Japan, Mexico, France, and much of Southern Europe and Asia. Here you "circle around" the stranger, getting to know him diffusely, and only come down to the specifics of the business later when relationships of trust have been established. On the right, you get straight to the point, to the neutral, objective aspects of the business deal, and if the other party remains interested, then you circle around, getting to know them in order to facilitate the deal.

Both approaches claim to save time. In the diffuse approach, you do not get trapped in an eight-year relationship with a dishonest partner because you detect any unsavory aspects early on. In the specific approach, you do not waste time wining and dining a person who is not fully committed to the specifics of the deal.

Specific and diffuse cultures are sometimes called **low** and **high context**. Context has to do with how much you have to know before effective communication can occur; how much shared knowledge is taken for granted by those in conversation with each other; how

FIGURE 7–4
Circling Round or Getting Straight to the Point

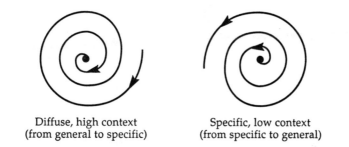

Diffuse, high context
(from general to specific)

Specific, low context
(from specific to general)

much reference there is to tacit common ground. Cultures with high context, like Japan and France, believe that strangers must be filled in before business can be properly discussed. Cultures with low context, like America or the Netherlands, believe that each stranger should share in rule making, and the fewer initial structures there are, the better.

Low-context cultures tend to be adaptable and flexible. High-context cultures are rich and subtle, but carry a lot of "baggage" and may never really be comfortable for foreigners who are not fully assimilated. There is growing evidence, for example, that Westerners working for Japanese companies are never wholly "inside." It is similarly hard for outsiders to feel fully accepted within the richness of French culture, with its thousands of diffuse connections.

There is a tendency for specific cultures to look at objects, specifics, and things before considering how these are related. The general tendency for diffuse cultures is to look at relationships and connections before considering all the separate pieces. The configuration is circular.

THE EFFECT OF SPECIFIC–DIFFUSE ORIENTATION ON BUSINESS

That Americans choose MBO (management by objectives) and pay-for-performance as favorite devices to motivate employees testifies in part to their specific orientation. In MBO, you first agree on the objectives, that is, the specifics. Supervisor A agrees with subordinate B that B will work towards agreed objectives in the coming quarter, and that evaluation of his or her work will take as a benchmark the objectives agreed to. Good objectives satisfactorily achieved will make for a productive relationship between A and B. What could be fairer or more logical? Why would the whole world not agree to do this?

This system does not appeal to diffuse cultures because they approach the issue from the opposite direction. It is **the relationship between A and B that increases or reduces output, not the other way round.** Objectives or specifics may be out of date by the time the performance evaluation comes around. B may not have performed as promised, yet done something more valuable in altered circumstances. Only strong and lasting relationships can handle unexpected changes of this kind. Contracts and small print face backwards in such cultures.

Japanese corporate cultures, for example, use terms unfamiliar to westerners which are clearly aimed at putting the diffuse before the specific. They speak of "acceptance time," the time necessary to discuss proposed changes before these are implemented. They speak of *nemawashi*, literally binding the roots of shrubs and trees before transplanting them. This refers to extensive consultations before implementing changes. All these constitute "the circling around before coming to the point" which we saw in Figure 7–4.

Attributes of Diffuse Cultures

Pay-for-performance is not very popular in diffuse cultures because it arbitrarily severs relationships. It says, "You are solely responsible for what you sold this month," when, in fact, other salespeople may have helped you, and your superiors may have inspired you or instructed you to act in more effective ways. To claim most or all of the rewards for yourself denies the importance of relationships, including feelings of affection and respect for superiors and peers with whom you have diffuse contacts and shared private life spaces.

Norms like "do not mix business with pleasure" and "let's not talk shop" testify to the desire in some cultures to keep specific life spaces separate from each other. Arguably, it is harder to coerce

FIGURE 7–5
The Specific–Diffuse Circle

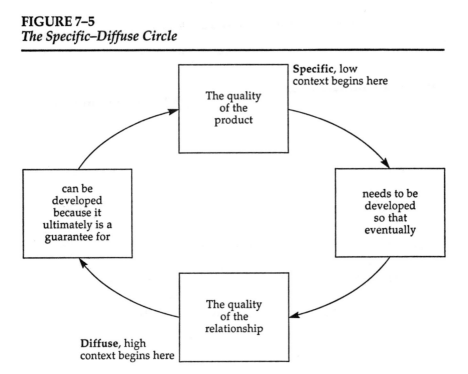

people or subordinate them if their lives are honeycombed with separate compartments. In this situation, only one area of somebody's life can be dominated, and they can call on the resources they have in other areas. Diffuse cultures have "all their eggs in one basket." Again, we are talking about **relative** separation, not absolute. There are always Chinese walls, at least, between life spaces in most cultures.

Diffuse cultures tend to have lower turnover and employee mobility because of the importance of loyalty and the multiplicity of human bonds. They tend not to headhunt or lure away employees from other companies with high (specific) salaries. Takeovers are rarer in diffuse cultures because of the disruption caused to relationships, and because shareholders (often banks) have longer-term relationships and cross-holdings in each other's companies and are less motivated by the price of shares.

Pitfalls of Evaluation and Assessment

Specific cultures find it much easier to criticize people without devastating the whole life space of the target of that criticism. There are at least two tragic corporate cases where criticism during performance evaluations by western superiors led to their murder by outraged targets.

In one case, a Dutch doctor whose job was to evaluate a Chinese subordinate in the company clinic had a frank discussion of the latter's shortcomings. In his view, these could easily be remedied by the company's training courses. Yet to the Chinese doctor, who had worked closely with the Dutch doctor and whom he regarded as a father figure, the criticism was a savage indictment, a total rejection, and a betrayal of mutual confidence. The next morning, he knifed his critic to death. It is easy to imagine the Dutch ghost protesting that he had never said his Chinese colleague was not a great fellow; it was only his medicine he was worried about.

In a second case, a British manager who fired an employee in Central Africa was later poisoned, with the seeming connivance of the other African employees. The fired man had a large number of hungry children, and he had stolen meat from the company cafeteria. In a diffuse culture, stealing is not easily separable from domestic circumstances, and the Western habit of separating an "office crime" from a "problem at home" is not accepted.

We must be careful, however, not to regard diffuse cultures as primitive. Japanese corporations give bigger salaries to workers with larger families, help in search for housing, and often provide recreation facilities, vacations, and consumer products at favorable prices. Another pair of questions we use to test for cultural diffuseness is the following.

   A. Some people think a company is usually responsible for the housing of its employees. Therefore, a company has to assist an employee in finding housing.
   B. Other people think the responsibility for housing should be carried by the employee alone. It is so much to the good if the company helps.

Figure 7–6 shows the percentage of managers who do not think that housing is a company's responsibility. Only 45 percent of Japanese managers think that it is not, as opposed to 85 percent of

FIGURE 7–6
Should the Company Provide Housing?

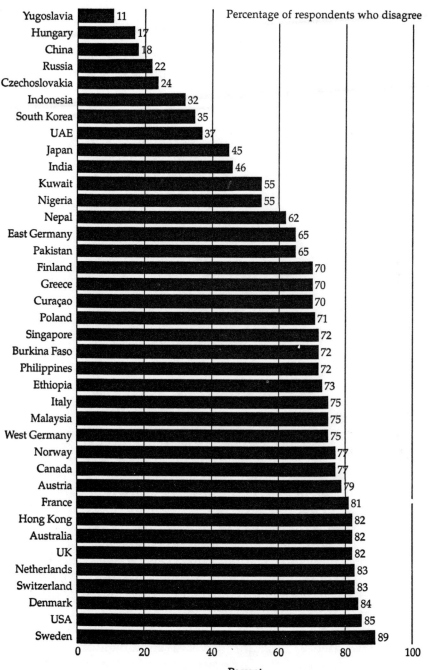

Percentage of respondents who disagree

Country	Percent
Yugoslavia	11
Hungary	17
China	18
Russia	22
Czechoslovakia	24
Indonesia	32
South Korea	35
UAE	37
Japan	45
India	46
Kuwait	55
Nigeria	55
Nepal	62
East Germany	65
Pakistan	65
Finland	70
Greece	70
Curaçao	70
Poland	71
Singapore	72
Burkina Faso	72
Philippines	72
Ethiopia	73
Italy	75
Malaysia	75
West Germany	75
Norway	77
Canada	77
Austria	79
France	81
Hong Kong	82
Australia	82
UK	82
Netherlands	83
Switzerland	83
Denmark	84
USA	85
Sweden	89

Percent

Americans. The great majority of all North European managers do not expect company help, but in most Asian countries the majority do. The exception is Singapore, where Western principles have become much more widespread. It is also interesting to note the impact of communist regimes on the various European countries which appear at the top of the chart.

Japanese consumers may reject Western imported goods because their value is specific; Japanese corporations produce goods with benefits diffused through their society. So we buy more than a Honda motor scooter; we "buy" economic and social development for our society, a highly diffuse concept.

THE MIX OF EMOTION AND INVOLVEMENT

There are, of course, various combinations of levels of emotion or affectivity (high to low, or neutral) with its reach or scope (diffusing several life spaces or remaining specific). A business partner can be emotional and expressive, yet not be involved **with you**. He may be cool and neutral, yet deeply involved in your private spaces. He can be expressive and involved, or neutral and uninvolved. Four combinations are described by Talcott Parsons,[3] which as Figure 7–7 shows, yield four different primary responses.

In diffuse–affective (DA) interactions, the expected relational reward is **love**, a strongly expressed pleasure diffusing many life spaces. In diffuse–neutral (DN) interactions, the expected reward is **esteem**, a less strongly expressed admiration also spread over many life spaces. In specific–affective (SA) interactions, the expected reward is **enjoyment**, a strongly expressed pleasure specific to a certain occasion or performance. In specific–neutral (SN) interactions, the expected reward is **approval**, a job-, task-, or occasion-specific expression of positive, yet neutral, approbation.

Of course, these four quadrants might also contain negative evaluations, **hate** (DA), **disappointment** (DN), **rejection** (SA), and **criticism** (SN). It is important to remember that love and responsiveness have their mirrors in hate and rejection, while more neutral cultures do not risk such extreme mood swings.

We have tried to measure the relative national preferences for love, esteem, enjoyment, and approval by using the following question, which is taken from some earlier work by L. R. Dean.[4]

FIGURE 7–7
The Emotional Quadrant

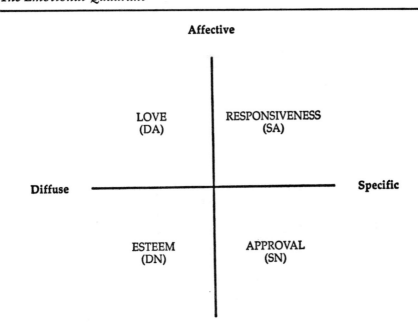

Source: Adapted with the permission of The Free Press, a Division of Macmillan, Inc. from *The Social System* by Talcott Parsons. Copyright © 1951, 1979 by Talcott Parsons.

Here are four general types of people we see around us in our daily lives. Review these descriptions carefully, then circle the one that most closely resembles you, as you actually are. Put a check beside the one you would like most to resemble, then two checks beside the one you would next most like to resemble.

  A. A person who is **esteemed** by others, and takes a continuous interest in human welfare in general.
  B. A person who is **enjoyed** by others, and takes their joys and sorrows as they come from day to day.
  C. A person who is **loved** by others, and takes a continuous interest in the personal welfare of all those who are dear to them.
  D. A person who is **approved** of by others, and attends to their affairs conscientiously from day to day.

FIGURE 7–8
Who Would You Like to Be? (Answers to Questions A–D on Esteem versus Love)

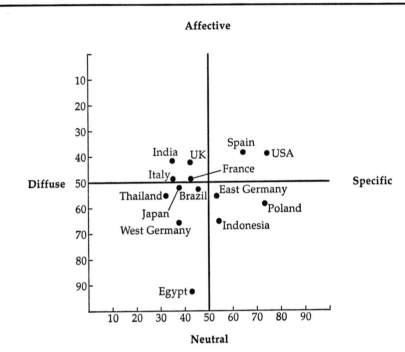

Figure 7–8 shows how a number of nationalities score in this exercise.

We see that a typical American approach is quite close to the mean both for emotion and in balance between the specific and the diffuse. East and West Germans are very similar in emotional levels, but East Germans are appreciably more specific, if not as specific as the Poles or the Japanese. Once again, there are no very clear rules by continent, although if we try to picture the most important regional cultural differences, we get the following division.

American (West Coast) enthusiasms tend to be for specific issues and causes, and belong, as it were, in separate boxes, that is, saving the redwoods, spiritual renewal, mamotechnology, virtual reality, and so on. DA cultures spill over between life spaces. Dishonor to one member of a family disgraces the family and must be avenged.

FIGURE 7–9
Regional Cultural Differences

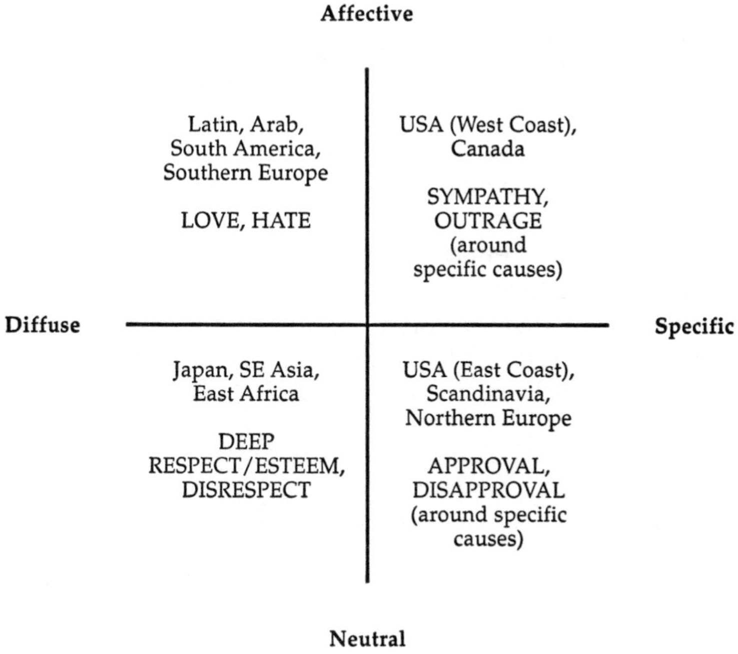

Affective

Latin, Arab, South America, Southern Europe LOVE, HATE	USA (West Coast), Canada SYMPATHY, OUTRAGE (around specific causes)
Diffuse	**Specific**
Japan, SE Asia, East Africa DEEP RESPECT/ESTEEM, DISRESPECT	USA (East Coast), Scandinavia, Northern Europe APPROVAL, DISAPPROVAL (around specific causes)

Neutral

You may not be able to work in the same company as a person with whom your uncle has a feud going back 10 years.

On one occasion, Dutch and Belgian managers disagreed on a fiscal issue in politics. The Dutch manager let the disagreement stand, in a separate compartment as he saw it, and tried to get on with other business. But for the Belgian, their disagreement colored everything. The Dutch manager could not be a trusted partner if his views on the fiscal issue were so mistaken. The Dutchman's desire to move on to other business was a slight to the Belgian's feeling of profound disturbance in their relationship. Their business dealings were broken off.

North Europeans, especially Scandinavians, are somewhat less specific than Americans, but are more disapproving of overt emotion. Like the Japanese, however, they sanction alcohol to loosen inhibitions. The lack of explicit emotion does not mean that people do not feel for each other. It means that a soft pedal is used to communicate emotions, but these small signs can, of course, speak volumes to the recipient who understands how to read them.

RECONCILING SPECIFIC–DIFFUSE CULTURES

This is perhaps the area in which balance is most crucial, from both a personal and a corporate point of view. The specific extreme can lead to disruption, and the diffuse extreme to a lack of perspective; a collision between them results in paralysis. It is the interplay of the two approaches which is the most fruitful, recognizing that privacy is necessary, but that complete separation of private life leads to alienation and superficiality; that business is business, but stable and deep relationships mean strong affiliations.

PRACTICAL TIPS FOR DOING BUSINESS IN SPECIFIC AND DIFFUSE CULTURES

Recognizing the Differences

Specificity	Diffuseness
1. Direct, to the point, purposeful in relating.	1. Indirect, circuitous, seemingly aimless forms of relating.
2. Precise, blunt, definitive, and transparent.	2. Evasive, tactful, ambiguous, even opaque.
3. Principles and consistent moral stands independent of the person being addressed.	3. Highly situational morality depending upon the person and context encountered.

Tips for Doing Business with:

Specific-Oriented (for diffuse individuals)	Diffuse-Oriented (for specific individuals)
1. Study the objectives, principles, and numerical targets of the specific organization with which you are dealing.	1. Study the history, background, and future vision of the diffuse organization with which you expect to do business.
2. Be quick, to the point, and efficient.	2. Take time and remember there are many roads to Rome.

Tips for Doing Business with: *(concluded)*

Specific-Oriented *(for diffuse individuals)*	Diffuse-Oriented *(for specific individuals)*
3. Structure the meeting with time, intervals, and agendas.	3. Let the meeting flow, occasionally nudging its process.
4. Do not use titles or acknowledge skills that are irrelevant to the issue being discussed.	4. Respect a person's title, age, and background connections, whatever issue is being discussed.
5. Do not be offended by confrontations; they are usually not personal.	5. Do not get impatient when people are indirect or circuitous.

When Managing and Being Managed

Specific-Oriented	Diffuse-Oriented
1. Management is the realization of objectives and standards, with rewards attached.	1. Management is a continuously improving process by which quality improves.
2. Private and business agendas are kept separate from each other.	2. Private and business issues interpenetrate.
3. Conflicts of interest are frowned upon.	3. Consider an employee's whole situation before you judge him or her.
4. Clear, precise, and detailed instructions are seen as assuring better compliance, or allowing employees to dissent in clear terms.	4. Ambiguous and vague instructions are seen as allowing subtle and responsive interpretations through which employees can exercise personal judgment.
5. Begin reports with an executive summary.	5. End reports with a concluding overview.

REFERENCES

1. Lewin, K., "Some Social-Psychological Differences between the U.S. and Germany," in Lewin, K., ed., *Principles of Topological Psychology,* 1936.

2. Feiffer, J., *Hold Me,* Knopf, 1968.

3. Parsons, T., and E. A. Shils, *Towards a General Theory of Action,* Harvard University Press, Cambridge, Mass., 1951, pp. 128–33.

4. Dean, L. R., "The Pattern Variables: Some Empirical Operations," *American Sociological Review,* no. 26, 1961, pp. 80–90.

Chapter Eight

How We Accord Status

All societies give certain of their members higher status than others, signaling that unusual attention should be focused upon such persons and their activities. While some societies accord status to people on the basis of their achievements, others ascribe it to them by virtue of age, class, gender, education, and so on. The first kind of status is called **achieved** status, and the second **ascribed** status. While achieved status refers to **doing**, ascribed status refers to **being**.

When we look at other people, we are partly influenced by their track record (top Eastern Division salesman for five consecutive years). We may also be influenced by their:

- Age (a more experienced salesperson)
- Gender (very masculine and aggressive)
- Social connections (friends in the highest places)
- Education (top scholar at the Ecole Polytechnique)
- Profession (electronics is the future)

While there are ascriptions that are not logically connected with business effectiveness, such as masculine gender, white skin, or noble birth, there are some ascriptions which do make good sense in predicting business performance: age and experience, education, and professional qualifications. Education and professional qualifications, moreover, are related to an individual's earlier schooling and training, and are therefore not unconnected with achievement. A culture may ascribe higher status to its better-educated employees in the belief that scholarly success will lead to corporate success. This is a generalized expectation and may show up as a fast-track or management-trainee program that points a recruit to the top of the organization.

With the issue of status in mind, let us get back to the trials of Mr. Johnson, who we may recall is struggling with a walk-out by Italian managers. Mr. Gialli and Mr. Pauli left the room furious when their suggested modification to the pay-for-performance plan was called "a crazy idea" by Mr. Bergman from the Netherlands. In order to save the situation, Johnson has turned to shuttle diplomacy. Like a youthful Henry Kissinger (Johnson is only 35), he finds himself moving between the two parties to settle the dispute. He rapidly begins to feel less like Kissinger and more like Don Quixote.

The Italian managers were far from assuaged. One even referred unpleasantly to "the American cult of youth: mere boys who think they know everything." So when the Spanish human resources (HR) manager, Mr. Munoz, offered to mediate, Johnson readily agreed. It occurred to him that Spanish culture might be closer to Italian culture, apart from the fact that Munoz, some 20 years his senior, could hardly be accused of inexperience.

While hopeful that Munoz might succeed, Johnson was astonished to see him bring the Italians back into the conference room in minutes. Munoz was not, in Johnson's view, the most professional of HR managers, but he was clearly expert at mending fences.

It was at once apparent, however, that Munoz was now backing the Italians' call for modifications to the pay-for-performance plan. The problem as he saw it, and the Italians agreed, was that under the current plan winning sales people were going to earn more than their bosses. Subordinates, they believed, should not be allowed to undermine their superiors in this way. Mr. Munoz explained that back in Spain his salesforce would probably simply refuse to embarrass a boss like this; or perhaps one or two, lacking in loyalty to the organization, might, in which case they would humiliate their boss into resignation. Furthermore, since the sales manager was largely responsible for the above-average performance of his team, was it not odd, to say the least, that the company would be rewarding everyone except the leader? The meeting broke for lunch, for which Johnson had little appetite.

As we can see, different societies confer status on individuals in different ways. Mr. Munoz carried more clout with the Italians for the same reason that Johnson had less; they respected age and experience much more than the specific achievements that had made Johnson a fast-tracker in the company. Many Anglo-Saxons, including Mr. Johnson, believe that ascribing status for reasons other than achievement is quite archaic and inappropriate to business. But is achievement orientation really a necessary feature of economic success?

STATUS-BY-ACHIEVEMENT AND
ECONOMIC DEVELOPMENT

Most of the literature on achievement orientation sees it as part of modernization, the key to economic and business success. The theory goes that once you start rewarding business achievement, the process is self-perpetuating. People work hard to assure themselves of the esteem of their culture and you get *The Achieving Society*, as David McClelland, the Harvard professor, defined his own culture in the late 1950s.[1] Only nations setting out upon an empirical investigation of what works best, and conferring status on those who apply it in business, can expect to conduct their economies successfully. This is the spirit of Protestantism; the pursuit of justification through works which long ago gave achievers a religious sanction, and capitalism its moving spirit.

According to this view, societies which ascribe status are economically backward, because the reasons they have for conferring status do not facilitate commercial success. Catholic countries ascribing status to more passive ways of life, Hinduism associating practical achievements with delusion, and Buddhism teaching detachment from earthly concerns, are all forms of ascribed status which are thought to impede economic development. Ascription has been seen as a feature of countries either late to develop, or still underdeveloped. In fact, ascribing status has been considered "dangerous for your economic health."

To measure the extent of achieving versus ascribing orientations in different cultures, we used the following statements, inviting participants to mark them on a five-point scale (1 = strongly agree, 5 = strongly disagree).

   A. The most important thing in life is to think and act in the ways that best suit the way you really are, even if you do not get things done.
   B. The respect a person gets is highly dependent on family background.

Figures 8–1 and 8–2 show the percentage of participants who disagree with each of these statements. The countries in Figure 8–1 where only a minority disagree with "getting things done" are, broadly speaking, ascriptive cultures; very broadly speaking, because there are in fact only three societies—America, Canada, and

FIGURE 8–1
Acting as Suits You Even if Nothing Is Achieved

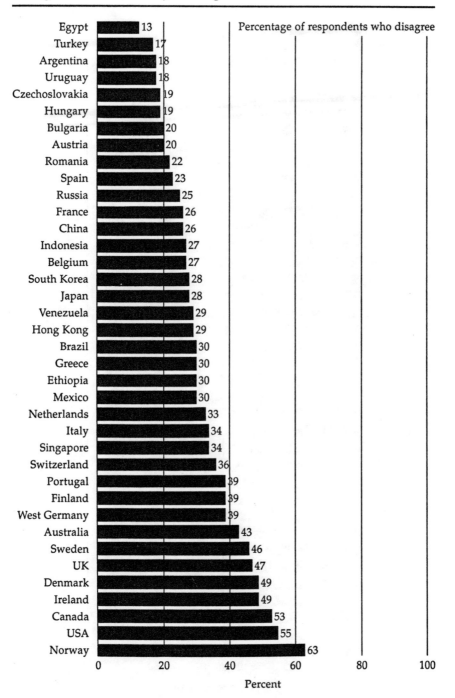

Percentage of respondents who disagree

Country	Percent
Egypt	13
Turkey	17
Argentina	18
Uruguay	18
Czechoslovakia	19
Hungary	19
Bulgaria	20
Austria	20
Romania	22
Spain	23
Russia	25
France	26
China	26
Indonesia	27
Belgium	27
South Korea	28
Japan	28
Venezuela	29
Hong Kong	29
Brazil	30
Greece	30
Ethiopia	30
Mexico	30
Netherlands	33
Italy	34
Singapore	34
Switzerland	36
Portugal	39
Finland	39
West Germany	39
Australia	43
Sweden	46
UK	47
Denmark	49
Ireland	49
Canada	53
USA	55
Norway	63

Percent

FIGURE 8–2
Respect Depends on Family Background

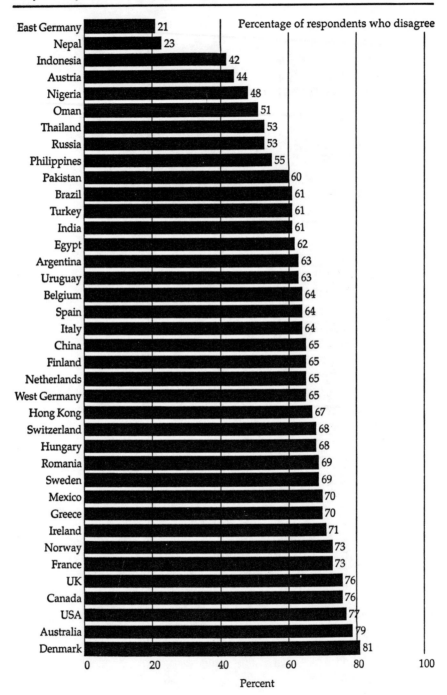

Percentage of respondents who disagree

Country	Percent
East Germany	21
Nepal	23
Indonesia	42
Austria	44
Nigeria	48
Oman	51
Thailand	53
Russia	53
Philippines	55
Pakistan	60
Brazil	61
Turkey	61
India	61
Egypt	62
Argentina	63
Uruguay	63
Belgium	64
Spain	64
Italy	64
China	65
Finland	65
Netherlands	65
West Germany	65
Hong Kong	67
Switzerland	68
Hungary	68
Romania	69
Sweden	69
Mexico	70
Greece	70
Ireland	71
Norway	73
France	73
UK	76
Canada	76
USA	77
Australia	79
Denmark	81

Percent

Norway—where there is a majority in favor of getting things done even at the expense of personal freedom to live as you feel you should. America is clearly a culture in which status is mainly achieved, as shown by Figure 8–2; 77 percent of Americans disagree that status depends mainly on family background. A number of societies which are ascriptive in the first figure (Italy, for example) do in fact show majorities against the proposition that status is largely dependent on family; aspects of ascription vary greatly from country to country.

Both figures show that there is a correlation between Protestantism and achievement orientation, with Catholic, Buddhist, and Hindu cultures scoring considerably more ascriptively. There is, incidentally, no correlation between support for achievement or ascription and the age, sex, or education of respondents across our database as a whole, although there is for these factors in some societies.

A second glance at the scores shows that there are growing difficulties with the thesis that an achievement orientation is the key to economic success. In the first place, Protestant cultures are no longer growing faster than Catholic or Buddhist ones. Catholic Belgium, for example, has a slightly higher GDP per head than the more Protestant Netherlands. Catholic France and Italy have been growing faster than the UK or parts of Protestant Scandinavia. Japan, South Korea, Taiwan, Singapore, and Hong Kong are influenced by Buddhism and Confucianism. It is certainly not evident that Japan's habit of promoting by seniority has weighed its corporations down beneath piles of dead wood. In short, there is no evidence that either orientation belongs to a higher level of development, as modernization theorists used to claim.

What appears to be happening is that some very successful business cultures are ascribing status to persons, technologies, or industries which they anticipate will be important to their future as an economy, with the result that these persons and sectors receive special encouragement. In other words, ascribing **works with** achieving by generating social and economic momentum towards visualized goals.

ASCRIPTION AND PERFORMANCE

Andrew, a British manager and trained geologist, had been working for a French oil company for 20 years and was still confused by one aspect of his colleagues' behavior. He found that his fellow

French geologists would simply not tolerate outside criticism of their profession. Initially he would get puzzled looks and frowns if he admitted he did not know the answer to some technical question in front of laypersons. Once when he said he would have to look something up, his French colleagues were overtly annoyed with him. He was confused because, in his view, geologists are frequently asked questions for which they do not have answers right at hand, or for which there is no answer. But his French fellows would chide him for admitting this publicly. They believed he was letting his profession down.

This experience is supported by research undertaken at INSEAD business school in France by André Laurent.[2] He found that French and Italian managers were much more emphatic about knowing all the answers than managers from many other cultures.

Notice, though, the effect that ascription has on performance. The French geologists are determined to live up to their ascribed status which, in turn, can lead to higher performance. Hence, it can be a self-fulfilling prophecy: through living up to the status ascribed to them, they deserve the status that was given to them before they actually earn it. In practice, then, achieving and ascribing status can be finely interwoven.

The European Community is a very good example of an ascribed self-fulfilling prophecy; its importance and power in the world was proclaimed before it had achieved anything.

The interweaving of ascribing and achieving orientations is a feature of the world's leading economies, Japan and Germany. Both cultures tend to confine achieving **as individuals** to the school days of their economic actors. Thereafter, managers are supposed to cooperate. Achievement becomes less a task for individuals jostling each other for advantage than for whole groups, led by those who excelled earlier and individually.

We must bear these distinctions in mind when we examine the data presented earlier. Ascribing and achieving can be exclusive of each other, but are not necessarily so. Your achieving can drive your ascribing, as when you "land winners." Or ascribing can drive achieving, as when key industries are first targeted and then won by "national champions."

The belief that electronic equipment made by Olivetti, Bosch, Siemens, or Alcatel is more important to the EC than enhanced expertise in distributing hamburgers or bottling colas is not entirely mistaken. You can ascribe greater importance to supposedly key industries on the basis of bad judgment or good judgment.

It is at least arguable that an economy needs to master electronics if it seeks to maintain competitiveness in manufacturing, since machines are increasingly monitored, controlled, and retooled electronically. You have a choice, then, of ascribing status to electronics **before** the achievements of manufacturing lapse, or **afterwards**. A culture that insists on waiting for dire results before changing course may handicap itself. Intelligent anticipation requires ascribing importance to certain projects, just as joint ventures, strategic alliances, and partnerships require us to value a relationship **before** it proves successful.

ACHIEVEMENT- AND ASCRIPTION-ORIENTED CULTURES' NEGOTIATIONS

It can be extremely irritating to managers from achieving cultures when an ascriptive team of negotiators has some *eminence grise* hovering in the background to whom they have to submit any proposals or changes. It is not even clear what this person does. He (usually male) will not say what he wants, but simply expects deference not just from you but from his own team, which is forever watching him for faint signs of assent or dissent.

It is, of course, equally upsetting for ascriptive cultures when the achieving team wheels on its aggressive young men and women who spout knowledge as if it were a kind of ammunition before which the team opposite is expected to surrender. It is rather like having to play a game with a toddler and a toy gun; there is a lot of noise coming from someone who is of no known authority or status.

Indeed, sending whiz-kids to deal with people 10 to 20 years their senior often insults the ascriptive culture. The reaction may be: "Do these people think that they have reached our own level of experience in half the time? That a 30-year-old American is good enough to negotiate with a 50-year-old Greek or Italian?"

Achievement cultures must understand that some ascriptive cultures, the Japanese especially, spend very heavily on training and in-house education to ensure that older people actually are wiser for the years they have spent in the corporation and for the sheer numbers of subordinates briefing them. It insults an ascriptive culture to do anything which prevents the self-fulfilling nature of its beliefs. Older people are held to be important **so that** they will be nourished and sustained by others' respect. A stranger is expected to facilitate this scheme, not challenge it.

Consider a Japanese–Dutch negotiating session. When Dutch experts in finance, marketing, and human resources meet their Japanese opposite numbers, the Dutch approach is to try to clarify facts and determine who holds the decision-making power. To the Dutch, the Japanese will appear evasive and secretive, not revealing anything. For the Japanese, these are not facts so much as mutual understandings between their leaders and themselves, which the Dutch seem to be prying into. This may come across as disrespectful. Anyway, it is for the leader of the negotiating team to say what these relationships are if he or she chooses to.

At a conference on a Japanese–Dutch joint venture held in Rotterdam, a Japanese participant fell ill. A member of the Dutch delegation approached Mr. Yoshi, another Japanese delegate with fluent English and outstanding technical knowledge, and asked if he would replace the sick man in a particular forum. Mr. Yoshi demurred, and the Dutchman was annoyed at the lack of a straight response. Several minutes later, the leader of the Japanese delegation, Mr. Kaminaki, announced that Mr. Yoshi would replace the sick man because Mr. Kaminaki was appointing him to the task. It was made very clear whose decision that had been.

The Translator's Role

In this and other negotiations, it often becomes clear that the translator from an ascriptive culture behaves unprofessionally according to the standards of achieving cultures. According to British, German, North American, Scandinavian, and Dutch values, the translator is an achiever like any other participant, and the height of his or her achievement should be to give an accurate, unbiased account of what was said in one language to those speaking the other language. The translator is supposed to be neutral, a black box serving the interests of modern language comprehension, not the interests of either party who may seek to distort meanings for their own ends.

In other cultures, however, the translator is doing something else. A Japanese translator, for example, will often take a minute or more to translate an English sentence 15 seconds long. And there is often extensive colloquy between the translator and the team he or she serves about what the opposite team just said. The translator on the Japanese side is an interpreter, not simply of language but of gesture, meaning, and context. His role is to support his own team and possibly even to protect them from confrontational conduct by the Western negotiators. He may protect superiors from rudeness and advise the team how to counter opposition tactics. The translator is very much on the ascribing team's side, and if the achievement-oriented team seeks flawless, if literal, translation, they should bring their own. This may not actually improve relationships because Asian teams are quite used to speaking among themselves in the belief that foreigners do not understand. If you bring someone fluent in their tongue, they will have to withdraw in order to confer. Your contribution to mutual understanding may not be appreciated.

The Role of Titles

The use of and mention of titles with business cards and formal introductions can be complex. This Dutch author carries three kinds of cards to introduce himself. In the Middle East and Southern Europe, formal titles received for formal education diffuse through several different contexts to elevate my status. In Britain, however, presenting myself as "doctor" may suggest a rather too academic bent for a business consultant. It may not be considered relevant for a consultant to have a PhD, and if attention is drawn to it, the status claimed is not necessarily legitimate. Achievement in a university may even disqualify a person from likely achievement in a corporation.

We might expect a similar situation in America, another achievement-oriented yet specific society. However, the inflation of qualifications in America makes it legitimate to draw attention to higher degrees from good universities, provided it is relevant to the task at hand. Typically, the specialty is mentioned: MBA, sociology, and so on.

In diffuse cultures, it is important to **tie in** your status with your organization. Indeed, your achievement as an individual will be discounted compared with the status your organization ascribes to you. It is therefore important to say not just that you are chief, but what you are chief of: marketing, finance, human resources, and so on. Many a deal has been lost because the representative was not seen to have high status back home. Ascriptive cultures must be assured that your organization has great respect for you and that you are at or near the top.

Relationship with Mother Company

In the value system of individualist, achievement-oriented cultures, the specific word of the representative pledges the company to any commitment made. The individual has delegated authority to use personal judgment.

In ascriptive cultures, the individual, unless head of the organization, almost never has the personal direction to commit the company without extensive consultations. An individual from an ascriptive culture may not really believe that the achieving representative has this authority either. Hence agreements are tentative and subject to back-home ratification. It is partly for this reason that your title and power back home are important to the ascriptive negotiator.

How can you deliver your company if you are not high in its status hierarchy? If you send an impetuous though clever youth, you cannot be very serious. It is important to send senior people if you are visiting an ascriptive culture, even if they are less knowledgeable about the product. It could also be important to ask for senior persons in the ascriptive culture to attend in person and meet their opposite numbers. The closer you get to the top, the more likely it is that promises made in negotiations will be kept.

Signs of Ascriptive Status Are Carefully Ordered

We are now beginning to see why pay-for-performance and bonuses to high achievers, whatever their rank, can be upsetting to ascriptive cultures. The superior is **by definition** responsible for increased performance, so that relative status is unaffected by higher group sales. If rewards are to be increased, this must be done proportionately to ascribed status, not given to the person closest to the sale. If the leader does something to reduce his own status, **all his subordinates are downgraded as a consequence.**

A British general manager, upon arrival in Thailand, refused to take his predecessor's car. The Thai finance manager asked the new GM what type of Mercedes he would like, then. The GM asked for a Suzuki or a Mini, anything that could be handled easily in the congested traffic in Bangkok.

Three weeks later, the GM called the finance manager and asked about prospects for the delivery of his car. The Thai lost his reserve for a moment and exclaimed: "We can get you a new Mercedes by tomorrow, but Suzukis take much, much longer." The GM asked him to see what he could do to speed up the process. After four weeks, the GM asked to see the purchase order for the car. The purchasing department replied that, because it would take so long to get a small car, they had decided to order a Mercedes.

The GM's patience had run out. At the first management meeting, he brought the issue up and asked for an explanation. Somewhat shyly, the predominantly Thai management team explained that they could hardly come to work on bicycles.

In this case, the status of each member was interdependent. Had the British GM ordered an even more expensive car, all the other managers might have moved up a notch. In ascriptive societies, you "are" your status. It is as natural to you as your birth or formal education (rebirth) through which your innate powers were made manifest. Ascribed status simply "is" and requires no rational justification, although such justifications may exist. For example, a preference for males, for greater age, or for social connections is not usually justified or defended by the culture ascribing importance to older men from "good" families. That does not mean it is irrational or without competitive advantage, however; it simply means that justifications are not offered and not expected. It has always been so, and if this means a major effort to educate staff as they age, that is all the better, but it is **not** the basis for preferring older people in the first place.

Achievement-oriented organizations justify their hierarchies by claiming that senior persons have achieved more for the organization; their authority, justified by skill and knowledge, benefits the organization. Ascription-oriented organizations justify their hierarchies by "power to get things done." This may consist of power **over** people and be coercive, or power **through** people and be participative.

There is high variation within ascriptive cultures, and participative power has well-known advantages. Whatever form power takes, the ascription of status to persons is intended to be exercised as power, and that power is supposed to enhance the effectiveness of the organization. The sources of ascribed status may be multiple, and trying to alter it by promotions on the grounds of achievement can be hazardous.

An achievement-oriented Swedish manager was managing a project in Pakistan. A vacancy needed to be filled, and after careful assessment the Swedish manager chose one of his two most promising Pakistani employees for promotion. Both candidates were highly educated, with PhDs in mechanical engineering, and in Pakistan both were known authorities in their field. Although both had excellent performance, Mr. Khan was selected on the basis of some recent achievements.

Mr. Saran, the candidate not chosen, was very upset by the turn of events. He went to his Swedish boss for an explanation. However, even an explanation based on the specific needs of the business did not calm him. How could this loss of face be allowed?

The Swedish manager tried to make the engineer understand that only one of the two could be promoted because there was only one vacancy. One of them was going to be hurt, even though they were both valued employees. He made no progress. The reason, as he eventually learned, was the fact that Mr. Saran received his PhD two years before Mr. Khan from the same American university. Saran was expected to have more status than his colleague because of this. His family would never understand. What was this Western way of treating ascribed status so lightly? Should not more than just the achievements of the past months be considered?

It is important to see how different the logics of achievement and ascription are, and not consider either as worthless. In achieving countries, the actor is evaluated by how well he or she performed the allocated function. Relationships are functionally specific; I relate to you as, say, a sales manager. The justification of my role lies in the sales records. Another person in that role must be expected to be compared with me and I with that person. Success is universally defined as increased sales. My relationship to manufacturing, R&D, planning, and so on, is instrumental. I either sell what they have developed, manufactured, and planned, or I do not. I **am** my functional role.

In ascribing cultures, status is attributed to those who "naturally" evoke admiration from others, that is, older people, males, highly qualified persons, and/or persons skilled in a technology or project deemed to be of national importance. To show respect for status is to assist the person so distinguished to fulfill the expectations the society has of him or her. The status is generally independent of task or specific function. The individual is particular and not easily compared with others. His or her performance is partly determined by the loyalty and affection shown by subordinates and which they, in turn, display. He or she **is** the organization in the sense of personifying it and wielding its power.

Achievement-oriented corporations in Western countries often send young, promising managers on challenging assignments to faraway countries without realizing that the local culture will not accept their youthfulness and/or gender, however well they achieve.

A young (aged 34), talented, and female marketing manager had worked for an American company in both America and Britain. She was so successful in her second year there that she was named the most promising female manager in Britain. This vote of confidence influenced her decision to accept an offer to transfer as director of marketing to her company's operation in Ankara, Turkey. She knew she had always been able to win the support and trust of her subordinates and colleagues.

The first few weeks in Ankara were spent, as usual in a new job, getting to know the local business, the staff, and how to get things done. Luckily, she knew one of the marketing managers, Guz Akil, who had been her marketing assistant in London. They had worked very well together.

Working as hard as she could over the first few months, she found her authority gradually slipping away. The most experienced Turk, Hasan (aged 63), informally but consciously took over more and more of her authority, getting things done where her own efforts were frustrated, although his marketing knowledge was only a fraction of her own. She had to watch him exercise influence, which most often led to unsatisfactory results. Through Guz, she learned that the head office complied with this arrangement, communicating more and more through Hasan, not her. She also heard that 10 years earlier, an American male manager the same age as her had been withdrawn for his inability to command local managers effectively. He was now working very effectively indeed for a competitor back in America.

When I presented this case in a workshop in San Francisco, pointing out the dangers of a universalist system for personnel planning, one female manager expressed concern. "You should not linger on this issue. You are advising us to discriminate on the basis of gender and age, or allow our overseas subsidiaries to do so. In this country, you could get sued for that."

Indeed, cultural preferences often have the force of law as well as custom. Refusal to send young women managers to Turkey because they are young and female is probably illegal, yet to send them is to confront them with difficulties which they may not have the capacity to surmount, through no fault of their own. The more they achieve, the more they seem to subvert the ascription process.

A better tactic can be to make a young female an assistant or adviser to indigenous managers. She will make up for any deficits in knowledge they have, while using local seniority to get things done. Such a posting could be paid and evaluated in the same way as being chief in an achievement-oriented culture, perhaps with a bonus for culture-shock. You cannot replace Turkish with American cultural norms if you seek to be effective in Turkey. This will not be effective in the long run, and in the short run can be very expensive.

TOWARDS RECONCILIATION

Despite far greater emphasis on ascription or achievement in certain cultures, they do, in my view, develop together. Those who start with ascribing usually ascribe not just status but future success or achievement, and thereby help to bring it about. Those who start with achievement usually start to ascribe importance and priority to the persons and projects which have been successful. Hence, all societies ascribe and all achieve after a fashion. It is once again a question of where a cycle starts.

PRACTICAL TIPS FOR DOING BUSINESS IN ASCRIPTION- AND ACHIEVEMENT-ORIENTED CULTURES

Recognizing the Differences

Achievement-Oriented	Ascription-Oriented
1. Use of titles only when relevant to the competence you bring to the task.	1. Extensive use of titles, especially when these clarify your status in the organization.
2. Respect for superior in hierarchy is based on how effectively his or her job is performed and how adequate their knowledge.	2. Respect for superior in hierarchy is seen as a measure of your commitment to the organization and its mission.
3. Most senior managers are of varying age and gender and have shown proficiency in specific jobs.	3. Most senior managers are male, middle-aged, and qualified by their backgrounds.

Tips for Doing Business with:

Achievement-Oriented (for ascriptives)	Ascription-Oriented (for achievers)
1. Make sure your negotiation team has enough data, technical advisers, and knowledgeable people to convince the other company that the project, jointly pursued, will work.	1. Make sure your negotiation team has enough older, senior, and formal position-holders to impress the other company that you consider this negotiation important.
2. Respect the knowledge and information of your counterparts even if you suspect they are short of influence back home.	2. Respect the status and influence of your counterparts, even if you suspect they are short of knowledge. Do **not** show them up.
3. Use the title that reflects how competent you are as an individual.	3. Use the title that reflects your degree of influence in your organization.
4. Do not underestimate the need of your counterparts to do better or do more than is expected. To challenge is to motivate.	4. Do not underestimate the need of your counterparts to make their ascriptions come true. To challenge is to subvert.

When Managing and Being Managed (concluded)

Achievement-Oriented	Ascription-Oriented
1. Respect for a manager is based on knowledge and skills.	1. Respect for a manager is based on seniority.
2. MBO and pay-for-performance are affective tools.	2. MBO and pay-for-performance are less effective than direct rewards from the manager.
3. Decisions are challenged on technical and functional grounds.	3. Decisions are only challenged by people with higher authority.

REFERENCES

1. McClelland, D., *The Achieving Society,* Van Nostrand, New York, 1950.
2. Laurent, A., *op. cit.,* see footnote 1, p. 163.

Chapter Nine

How We Manage Time

If only because managers need to coordinate their business activities, they require some kind of shared expectations about time. Just as different cultures have different assumptions about how people relate to one another, so they approach time differently. This chapter is about the relative importance cultures give to the past, present, and future.

Does an achievement-oriented culture believe that the future must be better than the past or present, since it is there that aspirations are realized? Does a relationship-oriented culture, on the other hand, see the future as threatening, likely to loosen current bonds of affection?

How we think of time has its own consequences. Especially important is whether our view of time is **sequential**, a series of passing events, or whether it is **synchronic**, with past, present, and future all interrelated so that ideas about the future and memories of the past both shape present action.

THE CONCEPT OF TIME

Primitive societies may order themselves by simple notions of "before" and "after" moons, seasons, sunrises, and sunsets. For educated societies, the concept of time is increasingly complex. Running through all our ideas of time are two contrasting notions: time as a line of discrete events, minutes, hours, days, months, and years, each passing in a never-ending succession; and time as a circle, revolving so that the minutes of the hour repeat, as do the hours of the day, the days of the week, and so on.

In the Greek myth, the Sphinx, a monster with the face of a woman, the body of a lion, and the wings of a bird, asked all wayfarers on the road to Thebes: "What creature is it that walks on four legs in the morning, two legs at noonday, and three legs in the evening?" Those unable to answer, she ate. Oedipus, however, answered "man," and the Sphinx committed suicide. He had grasped that this riddle was a metaphor for time. Four legs was a child crawling, two legs the adult, and three legs an old person leaning on a stick. By thinking in a longer sequence about time, the riddle was solved. He had also understood that, within the riddle, time orientations had been compressed or synchronized, and that language allows us to do this.

Anthropologists have long insisted that how a culture thinks of time and manages it is a clue to the meanings its members find in life and the supposed nature of human existence. Kluckhohn and Strodtbeck[1] identified three types of culture: present-oriented, which is relatively timeless, traditionless, and ignores the future; past-oriented, mainly concerned to maintain and restore traditions in the present; and future-oriented, envisaging a more desirable future and setting out to realize it. It is chiefly people in the latter category who experience economic or social development.

Time is increasingly viewed as a factor that organizations must manage. There are time-and-motion studies, time-to-market, just-in-time, along with ideas that products age, or mature, and have a life cycle similar to that of human beings. Uniquely in the animal kingdom, man is aware of time and tries to control it. Man thinks almost universally in categories of past, present, and future, but does not give the same importance to each. Our conception of time is strongly affected by culture because time is an idea rather than an object. How we think of time is interwoven with how we plan, strategize, and coordinate our activities with others. It is an important dimension of how we organize experience and activities.

When we create man-made instruments to measure time, we shape our experience of it. We can differentiate between duration and succession, and make fine distinctions within the compass of astronomical time, the time taken for the earth to revolve around the sun. We can think of time as fixed in this way by the motion of the earth, or we can think of time as experienced subjectively; on a jet aircraft, the position of the plane is sometimes shown on a map of the earth. We appear to be crawling very, very slowly towards our destination.

The experience of time means that we can consider a past event now (out of sequence as it were), or envisage a future event. In this way past, present, and future are all compressed. We can consider what competitive move to make today, based on past experience and with expectations of the future. This is an interpretative use of time.

Time has meaning not just to individuals but to whole groups or cultures. Emile Durkheim, the French sociologist, saw it as a social structure enabling members of a culture to coordinate their activities.[2] This has important implications in a business context.

The time agreed upon for a meeting may be approximate or precise. The time allocated to complete a task may be vitally important or merely a guide. There may be an expectation of mutual accommodation as to the exact time when a machine and its microprocessor are ready to be assembled, or there may be a penalty clause of thousands of dollars a day imposed by one party upon another. Intervals between inspections may be indicators of a manager's level of responsibility. Is he or she left for three months or three years to get on with the job? Organizations may look ahead a long way, or get obsessed by the monthly reporting period.

ORIENTATIONS TO PAST, PRESENT, AND FUTURE

Saint Augustine pointed out in his *Declarations* that time as a subjective phenomenon can vary considerably from time in abstract conception. In its abstract form, we cannot know the future because it is not yet here, and the past is also unknowable. We may have memories, partial and selective, but the past has gone. The only thing that exists is the present, which is our sole access to past or future. Augustine wrote: "The present has, therefore, three dimensions . . . the present of past things, the present of present things, and the present of future things."

The idea that at any given moment the present is the only real thing, with the past and future ceasing to be or yet to come, must be qualified by the fact that we think **about** past and future in the present. However imperfect our ideas about past or future, they influence our thinking powerfully. These subjective times are ever-present in our judgment and our decision making.

Although our lives may be consciously oriented to the future success of the enterprise, past experiences have deeply affected our perceptions of that future, as does our present mood. There is a potentially productive tension between the three, along with the ever-pressing question as to whether the future can benefit from past and present experiences (although companies, it is often remarked, have no memory).

All three time zones unite in our actions. It is as true to say that our expectations of the future determine our present, as to say our present action determines the future; as true to say that our present experience determines our view of the past, as to say that the past has made us what we are today. This is not juggling with terms, but describing how we think. We can make ourselves miserable in the present if a long expected payment is delayed to the future. We can discover in the present a fact that makes what we did in the past far more justifiable. In fact, an important part of creativity is to assemble past and present activities, plus conjectures about the future, in new combinations.

Different individuals and different cultures may be more or less attracted to past, present, or future orientations. Some live entirely in the present, or try to. "History is bunk," as Henry Ford put it, and inquiry into things past is best forgotten. Some dream of a world that never was and seek to create it from their own imaginings and yearnings, or they may seek the return of a golden age, a Napoleonic Legend reborn, a New Frontier similar in its challenges to the Wild West. They believe the future is coming to them, as a destiny, or that they alone must define it. Others live in a nostalgic past to which everything attempted in the present must appeal.

SEQUENTIALLY AND SYNCHRONICALLY ORGANIZED ACTIVITIES

We have seen that there are at least two images which can be extracted from the concept of time. Time can be legitimately conceived of as a line of sequential events passing us at regular intervals. It can also be conceived of as cyclical and repetitive, compressing past, present, and future by what these have in common: seasons and rhythms.

At one extreme, then, we have the person who conceives of time as a dotted line with regular spacings. Events are organized by the number of intervals before or after their occurrence. Everything has its time and place as far as the sequential thinker is concerned. Any change or turbulence in this sequence will make the sequential person more uncertain. Try jumping a queue in Britain. You will find that orderly sequence has very stern defenders. Everyone must wait their turn; first come, first served. It is part of "good form."

In London I once saw a long queue of people waiting for a bus when it started pouring rain. They all stood stolidly, getting soaked, even though cover was close by, lest they lose their sequential order. They preferred to do things right rather than do the right thing. In the Netherlands, you could be the queen, but if you are in a butcher's shop with number 46 and you step up for service when number 12 is called, you are still in deep trouble. Nor does it matter if you have an emergency; order is order.

Going from A to B in a straight line with minimal effort and maximum effect is known as efficiency. It has a major influence on the conduct of business in northwestern Europe and North America. The flaw in this thinking is that a straight line may not always be the best way of doing something; it is blind to the effectiveness of shared activities and cross-connections.

In a butcher's shop in Italy, I once saw the butcher unwrap salami at the request of one customer, and then shout, "Who else for salami?" The sequential idea is not entirely absent. People still pay in turn when they are finished, but if a customer has all she wants, she might as well pay and leave earlier than someone wanting additional cuts. The method serves more people in less time.

At my local butcher shop in Amsterdam, the butcher calls a number, unwraps, cuts, and rewraps each item the customer wants, and then calls the next number. Once I ventured the suggestion, "While you have the salami out, cut a pound for me, too." Customers and staff went into shock. The system may be inefficient, but they were not about to let some wise guy change it.

The synchronic method, however, requires that people track various activities in parallel, rather like a juggler with six balls in the air, with each being caught and thrown in rhythm. It is not easy for cultures which are not used to it. Edward T. Hall, the American anthropologist,[3] described what we call synchronic or **polychronic,** putting emphasis on the number of activities run in parallel. There is a final, established goal, but numerous and possibly interchangeable stepping stones to reach it. A person can "skip between stones" on the way to the final target.

In contrast, the sequential person has a critical path worked out in advance, with times for the completion of each stage. They hate to be thrown off this schedule or agenda by unanticipated events. In *The Silent Language*, Hall revealed that Japanese negotiators would make their major bids for a concession **after** their American partners were confirmed on their return flights from Tokyo. Rather than risk their schedules, Americans would often concede to the Japanese demands.

Synchronic or polychronic styles are extraordinary for those unused to them. I once purchased an airline ticket from a woman at a ticket counter in Argentina, who, while making out my ticket (correctly), was talking on the telephone to a friend and admiring her co-worker's baby. People who do more than one thing at a time can, without meaning to, insult those who are used to doing only one thing.

Likewise, people who do only one thing at a time can, without meaning to, insult those who are used to doing several things. A South Korean manager explained his shock and disappointment upon returning to the Netherlands to see his boss.

> He was on the phone when I entered his office, and as I came in he raised his left hand slightly at me. Then he rudely continued his conversation as if I were not even in the room with him. Only after he had finished his conversation five minutes later did he get up and greet me with an enthusiastic, but insincere, "Kim, happy to see you." I just could not believe it.

To a synchronic person, not being greeted spontaneously and immediately, even while still talking on the telephone, is a slight. The whole notion of sequencing your emotions and postponing them until other matters are out of the way suggests insincerity. You show how you value people by giving them time, even if they show up unexpectedly.

Sequential people tend to schedule very tightly, with thin divisions between time slots. It is rude to be even a few minutes late because the whole day's schedule of events is affected. "I'm running late," the scheduler will complain, as if he were himself a train or airline. Time is viewed as a commodity to be used up, and lateness deprives the other of precious minutes in a world where time is money.

Synchronous cultures are less insistent upon punctuality, defined as a person arriving at the agreed moment of passing time increments. It is not that the passage of time is unimportant, but that several other cultural values vie with punctuality.

It is often necessary to give time to people with whom you have a particular relation (see the discussion of universalism versus particularism in Chapter 4). It may be required that you show affective pleasure on meeting a friend or relation unexpectedly (see the discussion of the affective versus the neutral approach in Chapter 6). Your schedule is not an excuse for passing them by. Your mother, fiancée, or friend could be seriously offended.

Raymond Carroll, the French anthropologist,[4] tells of an American girl who left a note for her French lover. Could he let her know if he wanted to see her this evening, as if not she would like to make other plans? The Frenchman was offended. Her schedule should not get in the way of their spontaneously affective and particular relationship. People prominent in a hierarchy must also be given time if encountered (see status by achievement versus status by ascription in Chapter 8).

For all such reasons, meeting times may be approximate in synchronous cultures. The range is from 15 minutes in Latin Europe to part or all of a day in the Middle East and Africa. Given the fact that most of those with appointments to meet are running other activities in parallel, any waiting involved is not onerous, and late arrival may often even be a convenience, allowing some time for unplanned activities.

Even the preparation of food is affected by time orientations. In sequential, punctual cultures, exactly the right quantity of food will usually be prepared, and in such a way that it might spoil or get cold if the guests are not on time. In synchronic cultures, there is usually more than enough food in case more guests drop by unexpectedly, and it is either not the kind that spoils or else is cooked as wanted.

MEASURING CULTURAL DIFFERENCES IN RELATION TO TIME

The methodology used to measure approaches to time in this book comes from Tom Cottle, who created the "Circle Test."[5] The question asked was as follows.

> Think of the past, present, and future as being in the shape of circles. Please draw three circles on the space available, representing past, present, and future. Arrange these circles in any way you want that best shows how you feel about the relationship of the past, present, and future. You may use different size circles. When you have finished, label each circle to show which one is the past, which one the present, and which one the future.

Cottle ended up with four possible configurations. First, he found absence of zone relatedness. Figure 9–1 shows that, on our measurements, this is a typically Russian approach to time; there is no connection between past, present, or future, though in their view the future is much more important than the present and more important than the past.

The second Cottle configuration was temporal integration, the third a partial overlap of zones, and the fourth showed zones touching but not overlapping, hence not sharing regions of time between them. Figure 9–1 shows that this last approach is characteristic of the Belgians, who see a very small overlap between present and past, but the present and future as just touching. In this they are not dissimilar from the British, who have a rather stronger link with the past but see it as relatively unimportant, whereas the Belgians view all three aspects of time as equally important. Both are quite different from the French, for whom all three aspects overlap considerably; they share this view with the Malaysians and the Venezuelans. The Germans think the present and the future are very strongly interrelated. What the figure does not show is that half the Japanese see the three circles as concentric.

TIME ORIENTATIONS AND MANAGEMENT

Business organizations are structured in accordance with how they conceive of time. Corporations have whole departments given over to planning, to scanning the environment for new trends, to getting

FIGURE 9–1
Past, Present, and Future

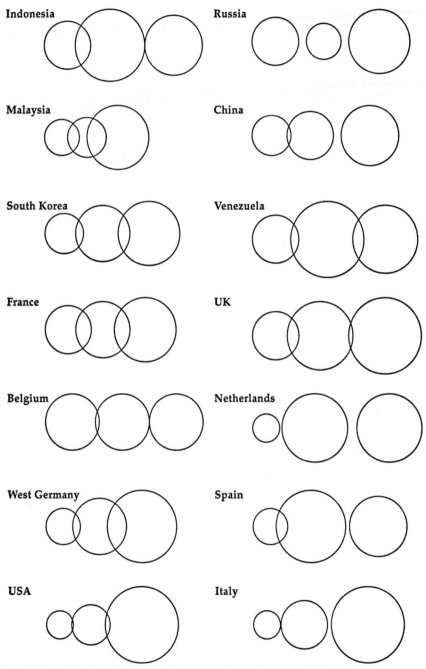

Source: Tom Cottle, "The Circles Test: An Investigation of Perception of Temporal Related-ness and Dominance," *Journal of Projective Technique and Personality Assessments*, no. 31, 1967, pp. 58–71.

production out faster, to shortening the time-to-market, that is, the time interval between a customer demanding a product and that product being designed, manufactured, and delivered.

Strategies, goals, and objectives are all future-oriented. Joint ventures and partnerships are agreements about how the future should jointly be engaged. Motivation is about what we can give to a person now so that he or she will work better in the future. Progress, learning, and development all assume an augmentation of powers over time, as does the habit of paying senior people more for the experience supposedly accumulated over time.

When orientations to time differ within corporations spanning different cultures, confusion can occur. Let us return to the sorrows of young Mr. Johnson of MCC. A good lunch makes even the most fundamental intercultural misunderstandings seem like ripples on a lake. Johnson had asked that the group reconvene at 2:00 PM precisely because they had a tight agenda for the afternoon.

At 1:50 PM, most participants returned to the meeting room. At 2:05 PM, Johnson started pacing restlessly up and down. Munoz and Gialli were still down the hall making telephone calls. They came in at 2:20 PM. Johnson said, "Now, gentlemen, can we finally start the meeting." The Singaporean and African representatives looked puzzled. They thought the meeting had already started.

The first point on the agenda was the time intervals determining bonuses and merits. All except the American, Dutch, and other Northwest European representatives complained that these were far too frequent. To Johnson and his Dutch and Scandinavian colleagues, the frequency was obviously right. "Rewards must closely follow the behavior they are intended to reinforce, otherwise you lose the connection." The manager from Singapore said:

"Possibly, but this go-for-the-quick-buck philosophy has been losing us customers. They don't like the pressure we put on at the end of the quarter. They want our representatives to serve them, not to have private agendas. We need to keep our customers long term, not push them into buying so that one salesperson can beat a rival."

The American view of the future is that the **individual** can direct it by personal achievement and inner-directed effort. This is why Johnson, backed by Dutch and Scandinavian managers, is keen to give pay-for-performance at regular intervals. Yet because the individual achiever cannot do very much about the **distant** future—there are simply too many events that could occur—America's idea of the future is short-term, something controllable from the present. Hence the accusation of "going for the quick buck" and the great importance given to the next quarterly figures. If the future is to be better, it is by steadily increasing increments of sales and profits. There is no excuse, ever, for not doing better now, since success now causes greater successes in the future.

It is interesting to compare the French respondents with the Americans. In French culture, the past looms far larger and is used as a context in which to understand the present. Past, present, and future overlap synchronously so that the past informs the present, and both inform the future.

I was once visiting the futuristic *La Défense* in Paris. As my French colleague was delayed, I picked up a brochure at the reception desk. It was about the company's achievements during the 1980s. I read it with interest and, as my colleague was further delayed, I asked the receptionist for a more recent one. She handed me the same brochure I had just read. She said it had been printed only two months ago and was the most recent available. Future opportunities for this company were very apparently connected to the success of the past.

Human Relations and Orientations to Time

Different orientations are also reflected in the quality of human bonds within an organization, and between the corporation and its partners. Any lasting relationship combines past, present, and future with ties of affection and memory. The relationship is its own justification, and is enjoyed as a form of durable companionship extending both far back and far forward. Cultures which think synchronously about time are more we-oriented (collectivist), and usually more particularist in valuing people known to be special.

The cultures concerned with sequential time tend to see relationships as more instrumental. The separation between time intervals seems also to separate means from ends, so that higher pay is the means towards still higher performance, and my customer's purchase is the means by which I will receive a higher bonus. The relationship is not entered into for its own sake, but in order to enhance the income of each party and the profit of the organization. The future looms large because present activity is but a means for realizing it. The important result is in the (near-term) future. Gratification is postponed because it will soon be greater.

Whether relationships unmediated by calculation of future gain are not closer and more amenable to dialogue is, of course, a very interesting question. Given the sheer complexity of modern business and the mounting volume of information that must be communicated, the durable, synchronous relationship in which the past, present, and future of the partners are bound together in co-evolution may be becoming a more effective way to manage. Certainly the idea that synchronous cultures are somehow primitive because their schedules are looser is not borne out. Sequential cultures, where human resources are seen as a variation on physical plant, equipment, and cash, are more likely to have we-them relationships or, to quote Martin Buber, "I-it."[6]

Time Orientation and Authority

In nations in which the past looms large and where time orientations overlap, status is more likely to be legitimized by ascription based on durable characteristics such as age, class, gender, ethnicity, and professional qualification. Past qualifications, for example at *les grandes écoles*, explain present eminence and promising futures, all of which are closely connected and synchronized.

On the other hand, when a person's career in Hollywood is "only as good as the last performance," the future is a sequence of episodes of relative success and failure. People will disencumber themselves of relationships and dependencies not useful in the next stage of their career, just as the original American immigrants cut off their roots. The authority of the individual will depend upon the latest achievement; those on the up today may be gone tomorrow.

Yet the authority of the individual can easily be challenged and assessed. What did they do in the most recent time interval? We find a reflection of this in the project-group organization pioneered by NASA and popular in North America and Northwestern Europe. Different parts of the organization are identified by and rewarded according to the fortunes in the future of the project being undertaken. Successes grow incrementally; failures are pruned back. Within the group, those contributing most to the project are also rewarded accordingly.

Policies of Promotion and Assessment

Sequential or synchronous cultures, and those concerned more with the past or with the future, may also assess and promote differently. In sequential cultures, the supervisor asks how the employee has performed over the previous interval. The more that employee can be held responsible for a rise or fall in fortune the better, and the supervisors will be tempted to minimize their own roles, or that of their relationship with the employee, since this does not help the employee to see his or her own recent achievement separated out as an increment of gain or loss.

In more synchronous organizations, on the other hand, the employee may be favorably assessed and promoted for the positive relationship established with the supervisors, who see that relationship developing over time and accumulating knowledge and mutuality. The supervisors gladly acknowledge their role in making the subordinate's career, as in the master–apprentice system in Germany.

MANAGING CHANGE IN A PAST-ORIENTED CULTURE

I was recently in Ethiopia with a Dutch manager who was terribly frustrated by his unsuccessful efforts to organize a Management of Change seminar with Ethiopian managers. They all kept harking back to a distant and wealthy era in Ethiopian civilization, and would not incorporate any developmental principles that were not based in this past.

After a discussion with Ethiopian colleagues, we decided to study some Ethiopian history books, looking at them from the perspective of modern management. What had Ethiopia done right in that period to make its cities and trade flourish? The company also had a rich history within Ethiopia, and these records too were studied. The Dutch manager posed the challenge anew. The future was now seen as a way of recreating some of the greatest glories of the past; suddenly, the Management of Change seminar had captured the enthusiastic support of everyone.

This is not a remote case applicable only to Ethiopia. All change includes continuity, that is, staying the same **in some** respects so as to preserve your identity. Many cultures decline to change at the behest of Western consultants unless the ways in which they will preserve their identity are made clear to them. Synchronic cultures carry their pasts through the present into the future, and will refuse to consider changing unless convinced that their heritage is safe.

A large American telecommunications company introduced a technically superior product on the world market. It planned to focus specifically on increasing sales in Latin America, where it had not been very successful previously. The only serious competitor was a French company which had an inferior product, but whose after-sales support was reputedly superior.

The Americans went to great pains to prepare their first presentation in Mexico. "Judgment day" would begin with a video presentation of the company and its growth potential in the medium–long term. After this, the vice president of the group would personally give a presentation to the Mexican minister of communications. Also meticulously planned was the two-hour lunch. Knowing Mexican culture, they believed this was where the battle would be fought. The afternoon session was reserved for questions and answers. The company jet would then be ready to leave Mexico City in the last departure slot. It was tight, efficient, and appreciated. Right?

Wrong. The Mexican team threw off the schedule right away by arriving one hour late. Then, just as the Americans were introducing the agenda for the day, the minister was called out of the room for an urgent phone call. He returned a while later to find that the meeting had gone on without him. The Mexicans were upset that the presentation had proceeded, that the after-sales service contract was separate from the sales contract, and that the presentation focused only on the first two years after installation, rather than the longer-term future together.

The French, on the other hand, prepared a loosely structured agenda. They determined some of the main goals to be attained by the end of the two-week visit. The timing, the where, and the how were dependent on factors beyond their control, so they left them open.

A long presentation on the historical background of the French state-owned company was prepared for the minister and his team. It had done business with Mexico's telephone system as early as 1930, and wanted to re-establish a historic partnership. As far as the French were concerned, the after-sales service, which extended indefinitely, was part of the contract. It was the French who received the order for a product known in the industry to be technologically less sophisticated.

What had gone wrong for the Americans? The main mistake was creating a tight, sequential agenda which was almost inevitably thrown off by Mexican officials who had deliberately built slack into their procedures and pursued agendas which were multiple and (to the Americans) distracting. The belief that the technologically superior product **should** win the contract is part of the original cultural bias in which each episode within a sequence is separated out. The Mexicans were only interested in the product as part of an ongoing relationship, an issue which the synchronous French were also careful to stress. Similarly, the Americans separated the after-sales service contract from the rest, presumably because it occurred at a later period. French and Mexican cultures see these time intervals as joined.

The French emphasis on the historic renewal of French-Mexican bonds was also effective with a culture that identifies with Spain and has deep European roots. American sequencing strikes synchronous cultures as aggressive, impatient, and seeking to use customers as stepping-stones to personal advantage. If the relationship is genuinely to last, what is the hurry?

Because the Mexicans did not agree that technological perfection was the key issue, they did not want to be on the receiving end of a detailed presentation timed to end just before the American departure. They wanted to experience a relationship they could partly control. In synchronous time, the demeanor of the American corporation during the presentation presaged its conduct in the future, and the Mexicans did not like it.

However, the biggest advantage the French had was their willingness to spend two weeks dedicated to an agreement, and leave it up to their hosts to use those two weeks in a flexible program aimed at synchronizing mutual efforts, rather than trying to agree to a schedule in advance. For the French and Mexicans, what was important was **that** they get to the end, **not** the particular path or sequence by which that end was reached. Similarly, the details of the equipment were less important to the Mexicans than the responsiveness of the supplier, since they could not know what problems might surface in the future. All they could really ask for, given this concern, was someone willing to alter a schedule to their convenience, and that the French showed they could do.

Moreover, the Americans had a narrower definition of how the negotiation should end. There should come a deadline when the Mexicans would say "yes." For the French, and synchronous cultures generally, there is no real "end"; the partnership continues. Instead of the **efficiency** of getting from A to B in the shortest possible time, there is the **effectiveness** of developing closer relationships long term.

The Americans also made one more serious mistake. Anticipating that the Mexicans would be late returning from lunch, as they had been several times, the Americans caucused for half an hour among themselves. This failed to show respect for the buyer. You give them time by waiting for them to join you. You do not use that time yourself in a way that makes you unavailable should they enter the room. A readiness to synchronize must be shown, as opposed to a mere delay in the sequence.

PLANNED SEQUENCES OR PLANNED CONVERGENCE?

In sequentially organized cultures, planning consists largely of forecasts, that is, of extending existing trend lines into the future and seeing this as "more of the same." Strategies consist of choosing desirable goals and then discovering by analysis the most logical and efficient means of attaining them. It is commonly believed that present and future are causally linked so that rewards now produce future achievements, which produce greater achievements, which produce greater rewards. Deadlines are important because they signal the end of one link in a causal chain and the beginning of the next, and keep you on schedule.

Planning varies considerably between sequential and synchronic cultures. In sequential planning, it is vital to get all the means or stages right and completed on time. "In Britain," an Italian female researcher told me, "everything needs to be planned from start to finish. When the environment changes, everything needs to be recalculated from the start." For the more synchronous Italians, the goals are what is most important, and the more paths you can devise to their realization, the better you fare against unforeseen events that block one path or another.

The 1990 *Mundialito* (Football World Cup) in Italy was an interesting example of Italian organization. The challenge was to complete the championships by a certain date on which the finals would be staged. To the dismay of the British and other Northwest Europeans, the Italians would periodically rejig the entire program to bring about this result. To the surprise of these other cultures, though, the Italians were able to pull it off. The 1992 Olympic games in Spain had many similarities with Italian planning.

There is accumulating evidence that sequential planning processes work less well in turbulent environments. They are too brittle, too easily upset by unforeseen events. The fact that they tend to concentrate on the near future testifies to the vulnerability of long sequences. Synchronic plans tend to converge or home in upon predetermined targets, taking into consideration fusions and lateral connections **between** trends that sequential planning often overlooks.

A most interesting example of a shift by a major corporation to a synchronic style of planning was the adoption by the Shell International Petroleum Corporation of **scenario planning**. In this exercise, scenarios for three alternative futures are written as if the writer was a contemporary commentator explaining how business had reached that point. In other words, past, present, and future are synchronized within the imagination, and three developments, traced from the past through the present into diverging futures, are written up as stories or narratives. For example, a scenario for 2003:

> In retrospect, it was inevitable that California would be the launching pad for the electric car. So polluted had the Los Angeles area grown, that the world's strictest emission standards, originating in the 1980s, led to partly electric cars in 1995 and the fully electric car eight years later. Slowly the pall began to lift. The final breakthrough was the "1,000 mile electric" with batteries that were rechargeable overnight. Was this, at last, the end of the internal combustion engine?'

In this type of planning, we see sequential and synchronous thinking combined. It proves possible to re-establish forecasts within the scenarios, so that each synchronous scene has a different sequence of events.

Once again, we find that differences in cultural orientation are not truly alternatives, but are capable of being used in conjunction. The wise cross-cultural manager perceives in **all** the ways preferred by different cultures. In scenario planning, sequencing and synchronizing work together.

PRACTICAL TIPS FOR DOING BUSINESS IN PAST-, PRESENT-, OR FUTURE-ORIENTED CULTURES

Recognizing the Differences

Past	Present	Future
1. Talk about history, origin of family, business, and nation.	1. Activities and enjoyments of the moment are most important (not mañana).	1. Much talk of prospects, potentials, aspirations, future achievements.
2. Motivated to recreate a golden age.	2. Plans not objected to, but rarely executed.	2. Planning and strategizing done enthusiastically.
3. Show respect for ancestors, predecessors, and older people.	3. Show intense interest in present relationships, here and now.	3. Show great interest in the youthful and in future potentials.
4. Everything viewed in the context of tradition or history.	4. Everything viewed in terms of its contemporary impact and style.	4. Present and past used, even exploited, for future advantage.

Tips for Doing Business

Past- and Present-Oriented	Future-Oriented
1. Emphasize the history, tradition, and rich cultural heritage of those you deal with as evidence of their great potential.	1. Emphasize the freedom, opportunity, and limitless scope for that company and its people in the future.
2. Discover whether internal relationships will sanction the kind of changes you seek to encourage.	2. Discover what core competence or continuity the company intends to carry with it into the envisaged future.

Tips for Doing Business (continued)

Past- and Present-Oriented	Future-Oriented
3. Agree to future meetings in principle, but do not fix deadlines for completion.	3. Agree to specific deadlines, and do not expect work to be completed unless you do.
4. Do your homework on the history, traditions, and past glories of the company; consider what re-enactments you might propose.	4. Do your homework on the future, the prospects, and the technological potentials of the company; consider mounting a sizeable challenge.

Recognizing Time Orientation

Sequential	Synchronic
1. Only do one activity at a time.	1. Do more than one activity at a time.
2. Time is seizable and measurable.	2. Appointments are approximate and subject to giving time to significant others.
3. Keep appointments strictly; schedule in advance and do not run late.	3. Schedules are generally subordinate to relationships.
4. Relationships are generally subordinate to schedule.	4. Strong preference for following where relationships lead.
5. Strong preference for following initial plans.	

When Managing and Being Managed

Sequential	Synchronous
1. Employees feel rewarded and fulfilled by achieving planned future goals as in MBO.	1. Employees feel rewarded and fulfilled by achieving improved relationships with supervisors/customers.
2. Employees' most recent performance is the major issue, along with whether their commitments for the future can be relied upon.	2. Employees' whole history with the company and future potential is the context in which their current performance is viewed.
3. Plan the career of an employee jointly with him/her, stressing landmarks to be reached by certain times.	3. Discuss with employee his/her final aspirations in the context of the company; in what ways are these realizable?

When Managing and Being Managed (concluded)

Sequential	Synchronous
4. The corporate ideal is the straight line and the most direct, efficient, and rapid route to your objectives.	4. The corporate ideal is the interacting circle in which past experience, present opportunities, and future possibilities cross-fertilize.

REFERENCES

1. Kluckhohn, F., and F. L. Strodtbeck, *Variations in Value Orientations*, Greenwood Press, Connecticut, 1960.
2. Durkheim, E., *De la Division du Travail Social*, 7th edition, 1960.
3. Hall, E. T., *The Silent Language*, Anchor Press, Doubleday, New York, 1959.
4. Carroll, R., *Cultural Misunderstandings: The French-American Experience*, University of Chicago Press, Chicago/London, 1987.
5. Cottle, T., "The Circles Test: An Investigation of Perception of Temporal Relatedness and Dominance," *Journal of Projective Technique and Personality Assessments*, no. 31, 1967, pp. 58–71.
6. Buber, M. (Kauffman, W., ed.), *I and Thou*, Scribners' Books, New York, 1970.
7. Shell International, Group Planning Department, London (personal communication).

Chapter Ten

How We Relate to Nature

The last dimension of culture we shall consider concerns the role people assign to their natural environment. This, like the other dimensions, is at the center of human existence. Man has from the beginning been besieged by natural elements: wind, floods, fire, cold, earthquakes, famine, pests, and predators. Survival itself has meant acting **against** and **with** the environment in ways to render it both less threatening and more sustaining. Constant action was originally an inescapable necessity.

Man's economic development can be viewed as a gradual strengthening of his devices to keep nature at bay. In the course of human existence there has been a shift from a preponderant fear that nature would overwhelm human existence, to the opposite fear that human existence may overwhelm and degrade nature, so that, for example, a genetic storehouse of incredible richness in the Amazon rain forest may be bulldozed to oblivion before we have even discovered it.

CONTROLLING NATURE, OR LETTING IT TAKE ITS COURSE

Societies which conduct business have developed two major orientations towards nature. They either believe that they can and should **control** nature by imposing their will upon it, as in the ancient biblical injunction to "multiply and subdue the earth"; or they believe that man is part of nature and must **go along** with its laws, directions, and forces. The first of these orientations we shall describe as **inner-directed.** This kind of culture tends to identify with mechanisms; that is, the organization is conceived of as a machine that obeys the will of its operators. The second, or **outer-directed,** tends to see an organization as itself a product of nature, owing its devel-

opment to the nutrients in its environment and to a favorable ecological balance.

American psychologist J. B. Rotter, working in the 1960s, developed a scale designed to measure whether people had an **internal
locus of control**, typical of more successful Americans, or an **external locus of control**, typical of relatively less successful Americans,
disadvantaged by their circumstances or shaped by the competitive
efforts of their rivals.[1] We used the questions he devised to assess
our 15,000 managers' relationships with natural events, and the answers suggest that there are some very significant differences here
between geographical areas. These questions all take the form of alternatives; managers were asked to select the statement they believed most reflected reality. The first of these pairs is as follows.

A. It is worthwhile trying to control important natural forces, like
the weather.

B. Nature should take its course, and we just have to accept it the
way it comes and do the best we can.

Figure 10–1 shows the percentage of respondents who chose A,
that is, the inner directors. No country produces a totally internal-
ized reaction to this statement; the highest score is only 53 percent,
but we see considerable variations between countries and, again, no
marked pattern by continent. Only 10 percent of Japanese believe it
is worth trying to control the weather, but as much as 43 percent of
Chinese; only 21 percent of Swedes, but 35 percent of the British.
The British, Germans, and Americans are above the middle of the
range, but by no means among the top scorers. If the alternatives are
made to appear more personally related, however, we get a different result. Figure 10–2 shows the percentage of respondents who
chose Question A when asked to choose between the following.

A. What happens to me is my own doing.

B. Sometimes I feel that I do not have enough control over the
directions my life is taking.

On this basis, a number of countries appear almost completely in-
ternalized. In America, for instance, 89 percent of managers believe
they control their own destinies, as do 82 percent of West Germans.
Most European countries score high, in fact, though not the East Germans, on whom 45 years of communism may have had some effect.
Similarly, the Chinese now rank much lower than the Japanese,

FIGURE 10–1
Controlling Nature

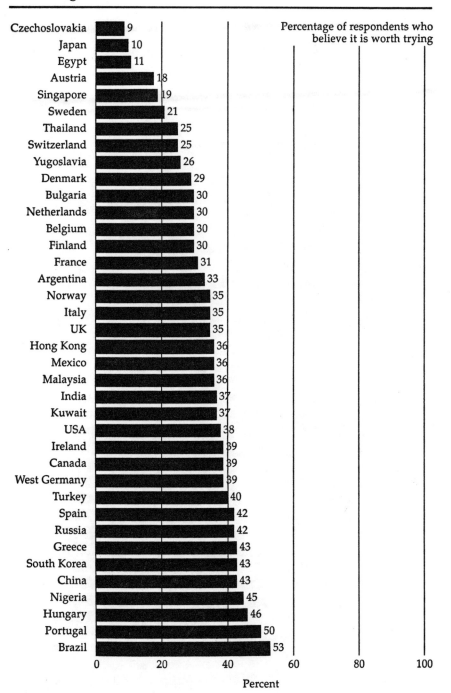

FIGURE 10–2
The Captains of Their Fate

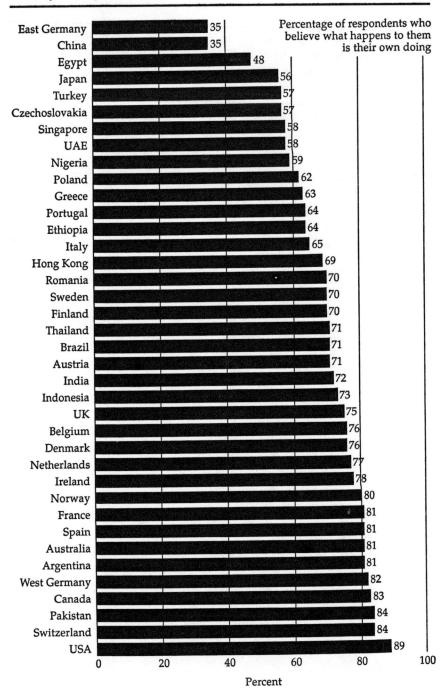

	Percent
East Germany	35
China	35
Egypt	48
Japan	56
Turkey	57
Czechoslovakia	57
Singapore	58
UAE	58
Nigeria	59
Poland	62
Greece	63
Portugal	64
Ethiopia	64
Italy	65
Hong Kong	69
Romania	70
Sweden	70
Finland	70
Thailand	71
Brazil	71
Austria	71
India	72
Indonesia	73
UK	75
Belgium	76
Denmark	76
Netherlands	77
Ireland	78
Norway	80
France	81
Spain	81
Australia	81
Argentina	81
West Germany	82
Canada	83
Pakistan	84
Switzerland	84
USA	89

Percentage of respondents who believe what happens to them is their own doing although in Japan, as in Singapore, managers are far less likely to believe in internal control than they are in North America or Europe.

CONTROL AND SUCCESS

The extremes of possible relationships between man and nature are perhaps best instanced by contrasting the ancient Greeks with 20th century Americans. For the Greeks, the world was ruled by natural godlike forces: beauty (Aphrodite), truth (Apollo), justice (Athena), passion (Dionysus). These forces would contend for human allegiance and were often in conflict, leading to tragedy. Virtue was to achieve *harmonia*, harmony among natural forces acting through you. Those who wanted their own will to triumph, like Oedipus or Jason, were frequently confounded in a struggle with their fates.

The post-Industrial Revolution society, on the other hand, has made heroes of entrepreneurs, whose struggles to tame nature are not expected to end in tragedy. This is especially the American view, shaped by the experience of discovering a new continent of immense size and small indigenous population, and turning a wilderness into a new nation. Success is identified with control over outside circumstances.

However, internal versus external loci of control do not necessarily distinguish the successful from the less successful in non-American cultures. There are ways of adapting to external influences which can prove economically effective. To accept direction from customers, market forces, or new technologies **can be more advantageous than opposing these with your own preferences.** The obvious advantages (to Americans) of being inner-directed may not be obvious at all to managers in Japan or Singapore, and will be at least less obvious in Italy, Sweden, or the Netherlands, for example. Outer-directed need not mean God-directed or fate-directed; it may mean directed by the knowledge revolution or by the looming pollution crisis, or by a joint venture partner. The ideal is to fit yourself advantageously to an external force.

In the original American concept of internal and external sources of control, the implication is that the outer-directed person is offering an excuse for failure rather than a new wisdom. In other nations, it is not seen as personal weakness to acknowledge the strength of external forces or the arbitrariness of events.

In outer-directed behavior, the reference point for actors lies outside themselves. A good example is the history of the Sony Walkman, already described in Chapter 1. In an interview in 1982, Akio Morita of Sony explained that he conceived the notion of the Walkman while he was searching for a way to enjoy music without disturbing others. This is in sharp contrast to the normal motivation for using a Walkman in Northwest Europe and America, where most users do not want to be disturbed by other people.

The preponderant inner-directness of North America and parts of Western Europe may help to explain why we have to go out of our way to teach customer orientation and "scanning the business environment." To outer-directed cultures like Japan and Singapore, this comes so naturally that they do not need to teach it. It is also noteworthy that outer-directedness does **not** preclude rivalry or competition, but rather can help to give it form and style.

To be directed by a customer or by the force of an opponent, as in Indo (Japanese wrestling) and Judo, is not to lack combativeness but to use another's powers in a more effective combination or harmony (*wa*). The word *do* in Judo, Indo, Kendo, and Bushido means "way of." You follow the way of the sword (Kendo) or the warrior (Bushido), their practices and disciplines, until they become part of your nature. You may, as a result, be a more formidable competitor, not less. Like a surfer, you respond to the waves and keep your balance when others lose theirs.

In contrast to many Eastern sports, in which the opponent's force is harnessed to your own, Western sports like American football or baseball idealize the zero-sum game, the clash of opposites, the rivalry of inner-directed wills, one-on-one. Only if you can't beat 'em should you join 'em. Even negotiations are won or lost depending on how much of what you originally wanted was gained, while compromise reduces the moral stature of all concerned.

Our Western contention that Asians steal our ideas is also shaped by our proprietary notions about what comes from **inside** of us and is therefore "ours." Asians may regard Western technologies as part of the environment, like fruit on a tree, which wise people pick and incorporate into themselves. Moreover, concepts such as *kaizen*, refinement, have very high cultural prestige. To take something from the external environment and then refine or improve it is not copying but celebrating that environment, letting the finest forces shape your character. Even when the forces are violent and humiliating, such as devastation, surrender, and occupation by Americans, the Japanese prove masters at adapting to external circumstances and emerging on top. As they like to say, "crisis is an opportunity."

Inner-directed Mechanism: The Renaissance Ideal

The West is heavily influenced by Copernican and Newtonian views of the universe as a vast perpetual motion machine which God wound up and left for His faithful to discover. To discover the laws of this universe, laws of time and motion, was to worship its creator. To understand the laws of the mechanism, it was necessary to predict and control the operation of nature's machinery, that is, to internalize natural law, and then show that nature obeyed you. Against this background, to be inner-directed has become proof of scientific veracity. We hypothesize and deduce, and the principle is correct if the predicted result follows. Enlightened man is the master mechanic, the driver with his hand on the throttle.

While the early physicists left the description of man to religious authorities, this division of labor broke down in the 17th and 18th centuries. Man, too, became a machine, using reason to drive a somewhat reluctant body to obey rational dictates. According to Jacques Ellul, the earlier belief in magic was now replaced by **technique,** applied not simply to external nature but to man's head and body. "Technique," writes Ellul, "is the translation into action of man's concern to master things by means of reason, to account for what is subconscious, make quantitative what is qualitative, make clear and precise the outlines of nature, take hold of chaos, and order it."[2]

After the Renaissance, then, nature became objectified so that manipulation could be more easily demonstrated over passive entities. Quantification and measurement became central to science, including social science.

The Modern View of Nature: The Cybernetic Cosmology

While for the Greeks nature was a living organism and for the Renaissance it was a machine potentially controllable by human reason, in modern system dynamics or cybernetics both these views

FIGURE 10–3
Changing Views of Nature

Era	Kind of Nature	Productive Functions	Philosophies	Focus of Control
Primitive	Organic nature	Arts: to form	Natural: natural world	External control
Renaissance	Mechanistic nature	Techniques: to transform	Mechanical: technical world	Internal control
Modern	Cybernetic nature	Applied sciences: to develop	Scientific: social world	Reconciliation of internal and external control

are transcended into a more inclusive concept of a living system which both nurtures the individual and can be developed by individuals dependent upon that system.[3] There is a shift from trying to seize control **over** nature to identifying with its ecological self-regulation and natural balance. The manager **intervenes** but is not the **cause** of what occurs; the systems of organizations and markets have their own momentum which we can influence but not drive. As the world fills up with economic actors and forces, we are simultaneously more influenced by external forces, yet more determined to create our own space among these.

Figure 10–3 summarizes these changing views.

HOW IMPORTANT IS A CULTURE'S ORIENTATION TO NATURE?

Orientations to nature have much to do with how we conduct our day-to-day lives and manage businesses. Cultures may seek to master nature, accept and be subjugated by it, or live in the most effective harmony with it. Nature is both controllable by man and liable to show sudden reversals of relative strength, becoming man's master, not slave. Neither situation is very stable nor very desirable, since a subjugated nature may fail to sustain man on earth.

A relationship closely analogous to man and nature is that of organization and markets. A product may succeed not simply because we will it to, nor because the special features designed into it delight customers. It may succeed for reasons **other than those which come from inside of us,** reasons which have to do with the way **other** people in the environment think rather than we ourselves. Are we then willing to take direction from customers, where this is not our original direction? Are we willing to change our minds when it becomes clear that customers' preferences are different from our own?

One powerful logic of outer-directedness is the theory of evolution. According to evolutionary biologists, it is the environment which decides which creatures fit and which do not, so, by extension, markets decide, not managers. The business world does not see the survival of the fittest, driven by mechanisms determined to outfight each other, but the survival of those best able to form a nurturant relationship with external niches and conditions. It may be for this reason that some outer-directed cultures are among the world's better economic performers. While the belief that the environment is all-powerful in deciding the future can lead to fatalism or resignation, the belief that we are all responsible can lead to scapegoating, blaming the victim, and a lack of compassion for those who have suffered misfortune.

An important aspect of inner-directedness is the notion of business **strategy,** that is, a plan designed in advance to wrest competitive advantage from other corporations. The metaphor comes from the military sphere, and it is clear that either the organization prevails in its strategic intention or it is bested by its environment.

The seeming lack of interest in strategy per se by the Japanese and similar outer-directed cultures has been noted, and the whole militaristic concept of strategy criticized, by Henry Mintzberg. Mintzberg points out that in any organization, those interfacing with customers have **already devised strategies for coping with day-to-day problems.**[4] The job of top management, therefore, is to take these emergent strategies and give recognition, status, and formal sanction to those which have proved most valuable. This is an outer-directed process for adopting strategies **already initiated** at the organization's grass roots, and is a further example of the need to let the environment shape **you.**

MANAGING BETWEEN DIFFERENT ORIENTATIONS TO NATURE

Paradoxically, Western and inner-directed managers trying to impose uniform procedures and methods on foreign and outer-directed cultures often succeed better than they expect, just because at least some of those cultures are accustomed to being heavily influenced from external sources and taking their cue from the environment. But it is a mistake to assume that **accepting** guidance from outside is the same as internalizing it or using it successfully. Some outer-directed cultures do not like to debate or confront, but this does not mean that the directive is appropriate to their culture. The source of authority is seen as natural, and will quickly be dissipated if the manager behaves in unnatural ways, for example by imposing his or her will for its own sake rather than because of a natural endowment of wisdom to sustain and nurture the organism. Other-directed cultures often regard nature as **benign.** If, therefore, you behave in ways interpreted as hostile, your natural powers will be forfeit.

At a Gabon subsidiary of a French oil company, I discovered that a new management program initiated by headquarters was failing miserably. The French managers, when interviewed, could not really explain what was going on. The Gabonese seemed to agree completely with the drafted mission statement. They even accepted the operational steps that had been discussed and planned at length. But when the plan had to be put into action, nothing happened. The employees behaved precisely as before.

After careful inquiry, it turned out that the Gabonese did indeed endorse the change, but did not believe that it was for them as individuals to direct its implementation. The signal had to come from their French superiors, who alone had the natural authority to command action. When no command came, no action was taken. The idea that self-directed change would emerge from reasoned principles was **not** culturally shared.

It was the same with the pay-for-performance program initiated by MCC. Such a program assumes that each employee can behave in ways that increase the sales of computers, that he or she can personally induce greater effort and hence greater sales. This assumption was questioned by an Asian manager.

Mr. Djawa from Indonesia raised two objections to Mr. Johnson.

"Pay-for-performance does not work in our sales territories. It leads to customers being overloaded with products they never wanted and do not need. Furthermore, when things are not going well for our people, it is a mistake to hurry them or blame them. There are good times and bad times. Paying them for performance does not change inevitable trends."

This did not impress Johnson and his Western colleagues. "We want to develop something at headquarters that will motivate everyone. Are you saying that linking reward to success has no influence at all? Surely you must agree there is some connection." Mr. Djawa said:

"It certainly has effects, but these tend to be swamped by economic booms and busts. Moreover, the customer needs to be assisted and protected from these fluctuations. It is not wise to push customers into buying more than they should. We need to ride out bad times together, and then take joint advantage of good times."

Many of Mr. Djawa's Eastern and Latin colleagues concurred. Mr. Johnson was exasperated. "Why don't some of you suggest a method that **does** work?"

Here the Indonesians, seeing themselves as relatively more controlled by external forces, seek to join with customers and each other to ride out the inevitable waves. They can be motivated, but in directions consistent with their culture, and that is to make skillful adjustments to the ups and downs which they experience as natural and not caused by their own greater or lesser determination to prosper. They seem to regard the turbulence of their environment as a sufficient challenge to the members of their organization, without needing to attribute blame to those caught in a downturn, or reward those caught in an upturn. To do either would sap group morale by adding to the arbitrariness of events and tempt sales personnel to put their own advantage ahead of the customers'.

In contrast, the mechanistic view of man sees the salesperson cutting through the waves like a ship heading for its own planned destination and not being diverted from its path by poor weather. The test of the good engineer or MBA is to do things right the first time and have their judgment vindicated by results. The good company promises "to put you in the driver's seat." Ideal mechanisms obey the will of their operators, and enable them to overcome natural obstacles to achieve personal goals.

IS MODERN MANAGEMENT A BATTLE
BETWEEN PRIVATE AGENDAS?

One problem with the inner-directed person seeking mastery over nature is that **everyone else** may come to stand for "nature." We all want power but can only achieve it if others are viewed as means to our ends. By definition, we cannot **all** direct the environment from within ourselves, since we ourselves constitute great parts of that environment. The invitation to others to participate is largely vitiated if, in fact, you are trying to steer them towards a conclusion you arrived at before the discussion began. Yet the relentlessly inner-directed manager has no other option. He or she is obliged to define social relationships objectively, as if moving pieces on a chess board. This is what Chris Argyris calls "Model I behavior," behavior designed to motivate the employee into doing what the manager formulated earlier.[5] Mr. Johnson, too, uses motivation in this sense, method of persuading salespeople to sell more in any or all circumstances and regardless of what they say or want, or what their cultures believe in.

The HAY method of evaluation of jobs is similarly inner-directed in identifying managers with their function. In this system, it is not the employee that is being evaluated, but the efficiency with which he or she completes a task assumed to be directed from within their supervisor, within their organization. It is this that gives authority its reason and legitimacy.

Suppose the company exists to turn natural raw materials into products. It requires these functions to be fulfilled by a division of labor. It hires people who agree to fill these functions. They are directed by a chief executive officer who personifies the organization's inner-directed purpose. Persons trying to fulfill these functions are then paid according to the complexity and difficulty of the function, how well they have discharged it, and how they used their own (inner-directed) judgment.

This is all logical, neat, and obvious, yet it treats physical and social environments as if they were objects, and is not the way large parts of the world economy think. It is also blind to some of the most obvious social facts, that during a conversation both parties may change their minds and transform their joint thought processes into something new and better.

SUMMARY

Cultures vary in their approaches to the given environment between belief that it can be controlled by the individual and belief that the individual must respond to external circumstances. We should not, however, make the error of assuming that inner-direction and outer-direction are exclusive options. All cultures necessarily take **some** notice of what is inside or outside. To fail to do so would lead inner-directed cultures into a headlong rush to disaster, while outer-directed cultures would try to please everyone and dissipate their energies by over-compliance.

Inner-directed managers are never happier than when they have won over other people to their own way of thinking. This is the ideal they strive for, but it is one which may be deemed aggressive and uncouth in outer-directed cultures. Leaders in these stress how much they have learned from their mistakes and from other's objections or criticisms. One reason staff suggestions enrich several Asian organizations and participation is so high is because listening rather than declaiming is seen as the more admirable trait. Such cultures do not clash openly. To negate what someone else is saying is to ride roughshod over nature. The alternative is to take the proposal on board and subsequently alter its import if it remains unpopular.

The word *feedback* is an interesting one in Western management jargon. It recognizes the need to correct periodically an ongoing thrust or function. But **rarely is feedback considered as important as that original direction.** Indeed, feedback is the means by which the original direction is **maintained.**

To participate fully in an outer-directed culture, inner-directed managers must accept that feedback can alter the whole direction of the organization. They must listen to the customers and aim to fill their needs as opposed to win their allegiance.

Major change can come from both outside and inside. Once again we see that culture is about where a circle starts or where a manager conceives of change originating. To conceive of the organization as an open system operating within a larger system allows both inner-directed and outer-directed orientations to develop.

PRACTICAL TIPS FOR DOING BUSINESS IN INTERNAL- AND EXTERNAL-ORIENTED CULTURES

Recognizing the Differences

Internal Control	External Control
1. Often dominating attitude bordering on aggressiveness towards environment.	1. Often flexible attitude, willing to compromise and keep the peace.
2. Conflict and resistance means that you have convictions.	2. Harmony and responsiveness, that is, sensibility.
3. Focus is on self, function, own group, and own organization.	3. Focus is on "other," that is, customer, partner, colleague.
4. Discomfort when environment seems out of control or changeable.	4. Comfort with waves, shifts, cycles if these are "natural."

Tips for Doing Business with:

Internally Controlled (for externals)	Externally Controlled (for internals)
1. Playing hard ball is legitimate to test the resilience of an opponent.	1. Softness, persistence, politeness, and long, long patience will get rewards.
2. It is most important to win your objective.	2. It is most important to maintain your relationship.
3. Win some, lose some.	3. Win together, lose apart.

When Managing and Being Managed

Internally Controlled	Externally Controlled
1. Get agreement on and ownership of clear objectives.	1. Achieve congruence among various people's goals.
2. Make sure that tangible goals are clearly linked to tangible rewards.	2. Try to reinforce the current directions and facilitate the work of employees.

When Managing and Being Managed (concluded)

Internally Controlled	Externally Controlled
3. Discuss disagreements and conflicts openly; these show that everyone is determined.	3. Give people time and opportunities to quietly work through conflicts; these are distressing.
4. Management-by-objectives works if everyone is genuinely committed to directing themselves towards shared objectives and if these persist.	4. Management-by-environments works if everyone is genuinely committed to adapting themselves to fit external demands as these shift.

REFERENCES

1. Rotter, J. B., *Generalized Expectations for Internal versus External Control of Reinforcement*, Psychological Monograph 609, 1966, pp. 1–28. (Some items have been designed by CIBS.)
2. Ellul, J., *The Technological Society*, Vintage, New York, 1964.
3. Moscovici, S., *Essai sur l'Histoire Humaine de la Nature*, Flammarion, Paris, 1977.
4. Mintzberg, H., *The Structure of Organizations*, Prentice-Hall, Englewood Cliffs, New Jersey, 1979.
5. Argyris, C., *Strategy Change and Defensive Routines*, Pitman, London, 1985.

Chapter Eleven

National Cultures and Corporate Culture

When people set up an organization, they will typically borrow from models or ideals that are familiar to them. The organization, as we explored in Chapter 2, is a subjective structure, and its employees will give meaning to their environment based on their own particular cultural programming.

The organization is like something else they have experienced. It may be deemed to resemble a family, or an impersonal system designed to achieve targets. It may be likened to a vessel which is travelling somewhere, or a missile homing in on customers and strategic objectives. Cultural preferences operating across the dimensions described in the previous chapters influence the models people give to organizations and the meanings they attribute to them.

This chapter explores four types of corporate culture, and shows how differences between national cultures help determine the type of corporate culture "chosen." Employees have a shared perception of the organization, and what they believe has real consequences for the corporate culture that develops.

DIFFERENT CORPORATE CULTURES

Organizational culture is shaped not only by technologies and markets, but by the cultural preferences of leaders and employees. Some international companies have European, Asian, American, or Middle Eastern subsidiaries which would be unrecognizable as the same company save for their logo and reporting procedures. Often these are fundamentally different in the logic of their structures and the meanings they bring to shared activity.

Three aspects of organizational structure are especially important in determining corporate culture:

1. The general relationship between employees and their organization
2. The vertical or hierarchical system of authority defining superiors and subordinates
3. The general views of employees about the organization's destiny, purpose, and goals, and their places in them

Thus far, we have distinguished cultures along single dimensions—universalism–particularism, for example, and individualism–collectivism. In looking at organizations, we need to think in two dimensions, generating four quadrants. The dimensions I use to distinguish different corporate cultures are **equity–hierarchy** and **orientation to the person–orientation to the task.**

This enables us to define four types of corporate culture, which vary considerably in how they think and learn, how they change, and how they motivate, reward, and resolve conflicts. This is a valuable way to analyze organizations, but it does have the risk of caricaturization. We tend to believe or wish that all foreigners will fit the stereotypes we have of them. Hence in our very recognition of "types," there is a temptation to oversimplify what is really quite complex.

The four types can be described as follows:

1. The family
2. The Eiffel Tower
3. The guided missile
4. The incubator

These four metaphors illustrate the relationship of employees to their notion of the organization. Figure 11–1 (page 154) summarizes the images these organizations project.

Each of these types of corporate culture are "ideal types." In practice, the types are mixed or overlaid, with one culture dominating. This separation, though, is useful for exploring the basis of each type in terms of how employees learn, change, resolve conflicts, reward, motivate, and so on. Why, for example, do norms and procedures which seem to work so well in one culture lose their effectiveness in another?

FIGURE 11–1
Corporate Images

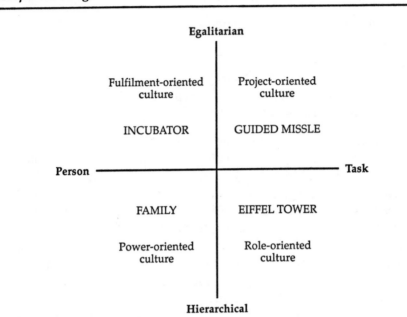

THE FAMILY CULTURE

I use the metaphor of family for the culture which is at the same time **personal,** with close face-to-face relationships, but also **hierarchical,** in the sense that the parents of a family have experience and authority greatly exceeding those of their children, especially where they are young. The result is a **power-oriented** corporate culture in which the leader is regarded as a caring parent who knows better than his subordinates what should be done and what is good for them. Rather than being threatening, this type of power is essentially intimate and (hopefully) benign. The work of the corporation in this type of culture is usually carried forward in an atmosphere that in many respects mimics the home.

Charles Hampden-Turner has pointed out that the Japanese recreate, within the corporation, aspects of the traditional family. The major business virtue is *amae,* a kind of love between persons of different rank, with indulgence shown to the younger and respect reciprocated to the elder. The idea is always to do **more** than a contract or agreement obliges you to. The idealized relationship is *sempai-kokai*, that between an older and younger brother. Promotion by age means that the older person will typically be in charge. The relationship to the corporation is long term and devoted.

A large part of the reason for working, performing well, and resolving conflict in this corporate culture is the pleasure derived from such relationships. To please your superior (or elder brother) is a reward in itself. While this affection may or may not be visible to outsiders (the Japanese, for example, are very restrained emotionally), it is nevertheless **there,** whether subdued in a Japanese style, or conveyed unmistakably by voice, face, and bodily gesture, Italian style. The leader of the family-style culture weaves the pattern, sets the tone, models the appropriate posture for the corporation, and expects subordinates to be on the same wavelength, knowing intuitively what is required; conversely, the leader may empathize with the subordinates.

At its best, the power-oriented family culture exercises power **through** its members acting with one accord. Power is not necessarily **over** them, although it may be. The main sanction is loss of affection and place in the family. Pressure is moral and social rather than financial or legal. Many corporations with family-style cultures are from nations which industrialized later: Greece, Italy, Japan, Singapore, South Korea, Spain. Where the transition from feudalism to industrialism was rapid, many feudal traditions remain.

Family-style corporate cultures tend to be **high context** (see Chapter 7), a term which refers to the sheer amount of information and cultural content **taken for granted** by members. The more in-jokes there are, the more family stories, traditions, customs, and associations, the higher the context and the harder it is for outsiders to feel that they belong or to know how to behave appropriately. Such cultures exclude strangers without necessarily wishing to do so, and communicate in codes which only members understand.

Relationships tend to be **diffuse** (see Chapter 7). The father or elder brother is influential in **all** situations, whether they have knowledge of the problem or not, whether an event occurs at work, in the canteen, or on the way home, and even if someone else present is better qualified. The general happiness and welfare of all employees is regarded as the concern of the family-type corporation, which worries about their housing, the size of their families, and whether their wages are sufficient for them to live well. The corporation may assist in these areas.

Power and differential status are seen as natural, a characteristic of the leaders themselves and not related to the tasks they succeed or fail in doing, any more than a parent ceases to be a parent by neglecting certain duties. Above the power of the leader may be that of the state, the political system, the society, or God. Power is **political** in the sense of being broadly ordained by authorities, rather than originating in roles to be filled or tasks to be performed. This does not mean that those in power are unskilled or cannot do their jobs; it means that, for such an organization to perform well, the requisite knowledge and skills must be brought **to** the power centers, thereby justifying the existing structure. Take the following testimony by a British manager.

> In Italy, I was introduced to my counterpart, the head of applications engineering. I asked him about his organization, his department, and the kind of work they were engaged in. Within minutes he had given me a dozen names and his personal estimate of their political influence, their proximity to power, and their tastes, preferences, and opinions. He said almost nothing about either their knowledge, their skills, or their performance. As far as I could tell, they had no specific functions, or, if they had, my informant was ignorant of these. I was amazed. There seemed to be no conception of the tasks that had to be done or their challenge and complexity.

It did not occur to the British manager that this family model is capable of processing complexity without necessarily seeing itself as a functional instrument to this end. The authority in the family model is unchallengeable in the sense that it is not seen to depend on tasks performed but on status ascribed. A major issue becomes that of getting the top people to notice, comprehend, and act. If older people have more authority, then they must be briefed thoroughly and supported loyally in order to fulfill the status attributed to them. The **culture works to justify its own initial suppositions.**

In my own research, I tested to what extent managers from different cultures saw their leaders as a kind of father, or to what extent they thought the leader got the job done. The results are shown in Figure 11–2, where we see one of the widest ranges of national variances of response, and a marked grouping of Asian countries towards the top of the chart. Another question asked of managers

FIGURE 11–2
What Makes a Good Manager?

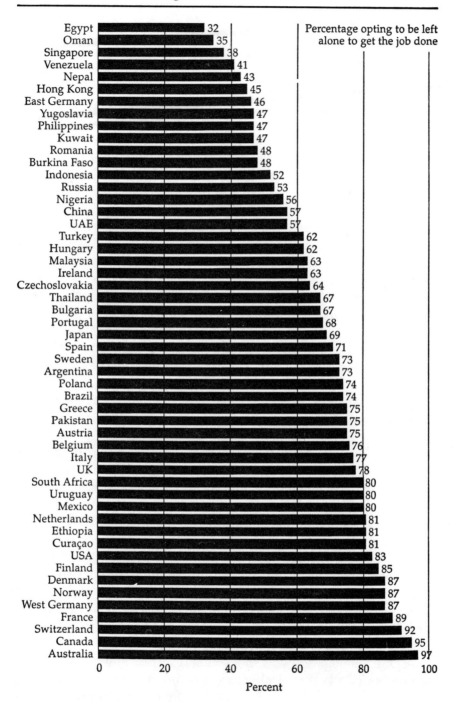

Percentage opting to be left alone to get the job done

Percent

in the process of this research was to think of the company they work for in terms of a triangle, and to pick the one in Figure 11–3 which best represents it. The steepest triangle scores five points, and so on down to one.

The scores of nations where the leader is seen as a person who gets the task done versus a kind of father (Figure 11–2) correlate closely with the steepness of the triangles in Figure 11–3. The familial cultures of Turkey, Venezuela, and several Asian countries have the steepest hierarchies; the image combines attachment to subordination with relative permanence of employment. Nearly all of these are also to be found in the top third of Figure 11–2.

Family cultures at their least effective drain the energies and loyalties of subordinates to buoy up the leader, who literally floats on seas of adoration. Leaders get their sense of power and confidence **from** their followers, their charisma fuelled by credulity and by seemingly childlike faith. Yet skillful leaders of such cultures can also catalyze and multiply energies and appeal to the deepest feelings and aspirations of their subordinates. They avoid the depersonalization of management by objectives; management by subjectives works better. They resemble the leaders of movements aiming to emancipate, reform, reclaim, and enlighten both their members and society, like the American civil rights movement; such movements also are essentially family-type structures, resocializing members in new forms of conduct.

Family cultures have difficulty with project group organization or matrix-type authority structures, since here authority is divided. Your function has one boss and your project another, so how can you give undivided loyalty to either? Another problem is that the claims of **genuine** families may intrude. If someone is your brother or cousin, they are **already** related to your family back home and should therefore find it easier to relate closely to you at work. It follows that, where a role or project culture might see nepotism as corruption and a conflict of interest, a family culture could see it as reinforcing its current norms. A person connected to your family at home **and** at work has one more reason not to cheat you. Families tend to be strong where universalism is weak.

A Dutch delegation was shocked and surprised when the Brazilian owner of a large manufacturing company introduced his relatively junior accountant as the key coordinator of a $15 million joint

FIGURE 11–3
Company Triangles

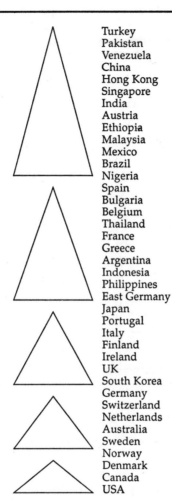

Turkey
Pakistan
Venezuela
China
Hong Kong
Singapore
India
Austria
Ethiopia
Malaysia
Mexico
Brazil
Nigeria
Spain
Bulgaria
Belgium
Thailand
France
Greece
Argentina
Indonesia
Philippines
East Germany
Japan
Portugal
Italy
Finland
Ireland
UK
South Korea
Germany
Switzerland
Netherlands
Australia
Sweden
Norway
Denmark
Canada
USA

venture. The Dutch were puzzled as to why a recently qualified accountant had been given such weighty responsibilities, including the receipt of their own money. The Brazilians pointed out that the young man was the best possible choice among 1,200 employees since he was the nephew of the owner. Who could be more trustworthy than that? Instead of complaining, the Dutch should consider themselves lucky that he was available.

The Eldest Child

Quite often, employees in family cultures will behave like the eldest child left in charge of the family while their parents are out, but relinquishing that authority as soon as a parent returns. The American manager of a plant in Miami, Florida, found this relationship with his Venezuelan second-in-command.

The plant processed and packaged polyvinylchloride (PVC). The process required high standards of quality control. The product had to be mixed in exactly the correct proportions or it was dangerous. Irregularity in mixing and blending had to be reported immediately and the line closed down at once, or unsaleable product would accumulate. A decision to shut down was an expert one requiring detailed knowledge. Even a delay of minutes was extremely costly. It was better on the whole to shut down prematurely than to shut down too late.

The Venezuelan deputy knew very well when the product was satisfactory and when it was not. When his manager was away from the plant and he was in charge, he would immediately stop any production line whose quality was failing. His judgment was both fast and accurate. When the manager was there, however, he would look for him, report what was happening, and get a decision. In the time it took to do that, considerable product was wasted. However many times he was told to act on his own, that his judgment was respected, and that his decision would be upheld, he always reverted to his original practice.

This was a simple case of a clash between the task orientation assumed by the American and the family orientation of the Venezuelan. The American had delegated the job of controlling the quality of PVC production. As he saw it, this was now his deputy's responsibility, whether he himself was in his office or away. It was required by the necessity of the process. But for the deputy, his authority grew when he was left in charge and shrank the moment his "parent" returned. Decisions should be taken by the most authoritative person **present.** He would no more usurp the authority of his parents once they returned home than would any child left temporarily in charge.

Some well-known research by Inzerilli and Laurent,[1] an Italian and a French researcher, showed the much higher regard among

Italian, French, and Japanese managers of the "manager who knows everything." This was on the basis of posing the question: "Is it important for a manager to have at hand precise answers to most of the questions raised by subordinates?"

We all know that, in the complexity of modern conditions, it is becoming harder for managers to know even part of what their subordinates know as a group. Yet the supposition that your manager **does** know everything may require you to discuss everything with him, thus encouraging the upward movement of information to the apex of the organization, a process that contributes to learning.

We must beware, therefore, of dismissing the family metaphor as primitive, pretentious, or feudal. Its intimacies can process complex information effectively, and wanting your "father" to know a great deal may have more desirable results than neither expecting nor wanting your boss to know very much. A visionary leader who mobilizes his or her employees around superordinate goals needs their trust, their faith, and their knowledge. The family model can often supply all three.

The results of the question posed in Chapter 7 on whether a company is responsible for providing housing (see Figure 7–6) also show those nations in which the family is a natural model. In these cultures, there is almost no boundary for the organization's responsibilities to the people in its employ. These even extend to where and how they are housed.

Japanese employers make it their business as to whether you are married, how many children you have, and, accordingly, how much more you need to be paid. The company may help you find housing, help get your children into schools, offer you consumer products at reduced prices, make recreational facilities available, and even encourage you to take vacations with work colleagues. The belief is that the **more the company does for your family, the more your family will wish its breadwinner to do for the company.**

Thinking, Learning, and Change

The family corporate culture is more interested in intuitive than in rational knowledge, more concerned with the development of people than with their deployment or utilization. Personal knowledge of another is rated above empirical knowledge about him or her.

Knowing is less hypothetical and deductive, more by trial and error. Conversations are preferred to research questionnaires, and insights to objective data. **Who** is doing something is more important than **what** is being done. If you invite the Japanese to a meeting, they will want to know who will be there before they ask specific details about the agenda.

Change in the power-oriented family model is essentially political, getting key actors to modify policies. Among favorite devices are new visions, charismatic appeals, inspiring goals and directions, and more authentic relationships with significant people. Bottom-up change is unlikely unless it is insurgent and seriously challenges the leaders, in which case major concessions may be made.

Training, mentoring, coaching, and apprenticeship are important sources of personal education, but these occur at the behest of the family and do not in themselves challenge authority but rather perpetuate it. Family-style cultures can respond quickly to changing environments that affect their power. Their political antennae are often sharp.

A Dutch manager delegated to initiate change in the French subsidiary of a Dutch group described to me how impressed he was at the precision and intelligence of the French managers' response to his proposals. He returned three months later to find that nothing had happened. He had failed to realize that it was also necessary to change the management team; the strategic proposals had simply been a front behind which the family continued to operate as before.

Motivating, Rewarding, and Resolving Conflict

Because family members enjoy their relationships, they may be motivated more by praise and appreciation than by money. Pay-for-performance, or any motivation that threatens family bonds, rarely sits well with them. They tend to "socialize risk" among their members and can operate in uncertain environments quite well. Their major weakness occurs when intra-family conflicts block necessary change.

Resolving conflict often depends on the skill of a leader. Criticisms are seldom voiced publicly; if they are, the family is in turmoil. Negative feedback is indirect and sometimes confined to special "licensed" occasions. (In Japan, you can criticize your boss while drinking his booze.) Care is taken to avoid loss of face by prominent family members, since these are points of coherence for the whole group. The family model gives low priority to **efficiency** (doing things right), but high priority to **effectiveness** (doing the right things).

THE EIFFEL TOWER CULTURE

In the Western world, a bureaucratic division of labor, with various roles and functions, is prescribed in advance. These allocations are co-ordinated at the top by a hierarchy. If each role is acted out as envisaged by the system, then tasks will be completed as planned. One supervisor can oversee the completion of several tasks; one manager can oversee the job of several supervisors; and so on up the hierarchy.

I have chosen the Eiffel Tower in Paris to symbolize this cultural type because it is steep, symmetrical, narrow at the top, and broad at the base, stable, rigid, and robust. Like the formal bureaucracy for which it stands, it is very much a symbol of the machine age. Its structure, too, is more important than its function.

Its hierarchy is very different from that of the family. Each higher level has a clear and demonstrable function of holding together the levels beneath it. You obey the boss because it is his or her **role** to instruct you. The rational purpose of the corporation is conveyed to you through him. He has legal authority to tell you what to do, and your contract of service, overtly or implicitly, obliges you to work according to his instructions. If you and other subordinates did not do so, the system could not function.

The boss in the Eiffel Tower is only incidentally a person. Essentially, he or she is a role. Were he to drop dead tomorrow, someone else would replace him, and it would make no difference to your duties or to the organization's reason for being. His successor might, of course, be more or less unpleasant, or interpret the role slightly differently, but that is marginal. Effectively, the job is defined and the discharge of it evaluated according to that definition. Very little is left to chance or the idiosyncrasies of individuals.

It follows that authority stems from occupancy of the role. If you meet the boss on the golf course, you have no obligation to let him play through, and he probably would not expect it. Relationships are **specific** (see Chapter 7), and status is ascribed (see Chapter 8) and stays behind at the office. This is not, however, a personal ascription of status as we see it in the family. Status in the Eiffel Tower is ascribed to the role. This makes it impossible to challenge. Thus bureaucracy in the Eiffel Tower is a depersonalized, rational-legal system in which everyone is subordinate to local rules, and those rules prescribe a hierarchy to uphold and enforce them. The boss is powerful only because the rules sanction him or her to act.

Careers in Eiffel Tower companies are much assisted by professional qualifications. At the top of German and Austrian companies, which are typically Eiffel Tower models, the titles of professor or doctor are common on office doors. This is extremely rare in America.

Almost everything the family culture accepts, the Eiffel Tower rejects. Personal relationships are likely to warp judgments, create favorites, multiply exceptions to the rules, and obscure clear boundaries between roles and responsibilities. You cannot evaluate your subordinates' performance in a role if you grow fond of them or need their personal loyalty for yourself. The organization's purpose is logically separate from your personal need for power or affection. Such needs are distractions, biases, and intrusions by personal agendas upon public ones.

Each role at each level of the hierarchy is described, rated for its difficulty, complexity, and responsibility, and has a salary attached to it. There then follows a search for a person to fill it. In considering applicants for the role, the personnel department will treat everyone equally and neutrally, match the person's skills and aptitudes with the job requirements, and award the job to the best fit between role and person. The same procedure is followed in evaluations and promotions.

I tested the influence of the **role** culture as opposed to the more **personal** culture by posing the following dilemma to managers.

Two managers talk about the organizational structure of their company.

- **A.** One says: "The main reason for having an organizational structure is so that everyone knows who has authority over whom."
- **B.** The other says: "The main reason for having an organizational structure is so that everyone knows how functions are allocated and coordinated."

FIGURE 11–4
The Reason for Organization

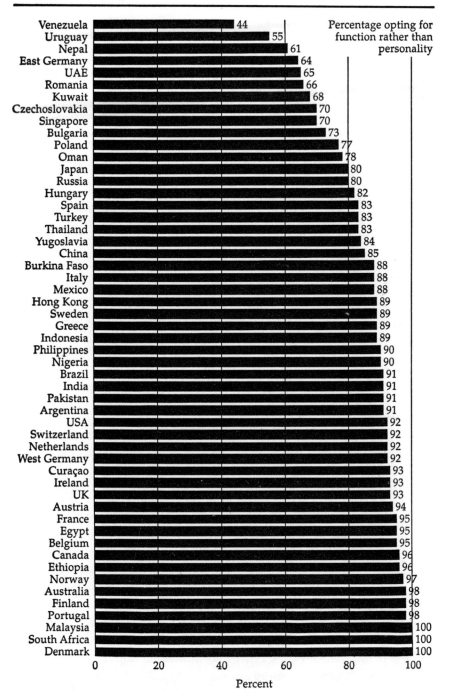

Percentage opting for function rather than personality

Percent

Which one of these two ways usually best represents an organizational structure?

Those nations most attracted to putting roles before persons, largely North American and Northwest European, opt by large majorities for B. Here the **logic of subordination is clearly rational and coordinative.** In option A, it is left unspecified. The organization legitimates existing power differences.

The Eiffel Tower points to the goals to be achieved by the edifice, which is relatively rigid and has difficulty pointing in different directions. If, for example, the Eiffel Tower company needs to achieve goals inconsistent with hierarchical coordinated roles, say inventing new products, then its structure tends to impede achievement. On the other hand, it is well designed to renew passports or check insurance claims, where the rules are devised in advance and consistent treatment is legally required.

In one of our workshops, the head of strategic planning in a major German company gave a one-hour presentation on his company's strategic planning. He spent 45 minutes on how his firm was organized, and the remaining 15 minutes on strategic issues. Over lunch, I asked him why he had not wanted to give 60 minutes to strategic issues. "But I did," was his reply. For him, structure **was** strategy.

Thinking, Learning, and Change

The way in which people think, learn, and change in the role-oriented Eiffel Tower company is significantly different from similar processes in the family. For employees in the Eiffel Tower, the family culture is arbitrary, irrational, conspiratorial, cozy, and corrupt. Instead of following set procedures which everyone can understand, and having objective benchmarks which employees agree to conform to, the family is forever shifting goalposts or suspending competitive play altogether.

Learning in the Eiffel Tower means accumulating the skills necessary to fit a role and, hopefully, the additional skills to qualify for higher positions. In Eiffel Tower companies, people, or human resources, are conceived of as similar to capital and cash resources. People of known qualifications can be planned, scheduled, deployed, and reshuffled by skill sets like any other physical entity. Manpower planning, assessment centers, appraisal systems, training schemes, and job rotation all have the function of helping to classify and produce resources to fit known roles.

Change in the Eiffel Tower is effected through **changing rules.** With any alteration in the company's purpose must come changes in what employees are formally required to do. For this reason, the culture does not adapt well to turbulent environments. In theory, constant rule change would be necessary, but this would in practice bewilder employees, lower morale, and obscure the distinction between rules and deviations. Change in an Eiffel Tower culture is immensely complex and time consuming. Manuals must be rewritten, procedures changed, job descriptions altered, promotions reconsidered, qualifications reassessed. Restructuring or rationalization tend to be dreaded words in Eiffel Tower cultures. They usually mean wholesale firings and redundancies. Such companies resist change, and, when it becomes inevitable, suffer major dislocation as a consequence.

An American manager responsible for initiating change in a German company described to me the difficulties he had had in making progress, although the German managers had discussed the new strategy in depth and made significant contributions to its formulation. Through informal channels, he had eventually discovered that his mistake was not having formalized the changes to structure or job descriptions. In the absence of a new organization chart, this Eiffel Tower company was unable to change. Like the Dutch manager above who had similar problems in dealing with a French family company, his assumption was that, once an intellectual decision had been agreed, instant action would follow. Both these managers came from task-oriented, guided-missile cultures themselves (see below).

Motivating, Rewarding, and Resolving Conflict

Employees of the Eiffel Tower are ideally precise and meticulous. They are nervous when order and predictability are lacking. Duty is an important concept for the role-oriented employee. It is an obligation people feel within themselves, rather than an obligation they feel towards a specific individual.

Conflicts are seen as irrational, as pathologies of orderly procedure, as offenses against efficiency. Criticisms and complaints are
typically channelled and dealt with through even more rules and
fact-finding procedures.

THE FAMILY AND THE EIFFEL TOWER IN CONFLICT

MCC, the company employing Mr. Johnson, whose problems we
have been following throughout this book, is, broadly speaking, a
task-oriented company, and many of Mr. Johnson's difficulties have
arisen through clashes with colleagues whose expectations of companies are much closer to the family model. (The final installment
of Mr. Johnson's story will be found at the end of this chapter.)

Another example of what happens when these two models find
themselves side by side is the story of Heinz, a manager from a large
German multinational. Experienced and outstandingly successful,
he was selected to help a Colombian packaging materials company
to get out of the red. All stakeholders, the Colombian government
included, acknowledged that modernization and more professional
management were needed. Heinz wanted to make the factory prof-
itable and more efficient by introducing new production and quality standards.

The most important person in the company next to Heinz was
Antonio, a Colombian who was designated to take over Heinz's job
after the German had completed his mission. After almost a year of
working in Colombia, Heinz concluded that the activities in the factory had not improved significantly despite his best efforts.

The following are excerpts from a consultant's report (rewritten
by Leonel Brug) in which Heinz and Antonio were interviewed separately.

Antonio's story. Antonio is very positive about Heinz's technical and
organizational capabilities. The need to increase efficiency is undeni-
able, and the production processes still need much work. Heinz is quite
right on this score.

Antonio is, however, shocked by the way Heinz is trying to impose
his methods and ideas on the Colombians. He describes this as turning
them into robots; he is dehumanizing the whole organization.

He says Heinz seems obsessed with time and money. People hardly count at all. He yells at workers for taking longer breaks than they should, forgetting that the previous week they worked overtime without extra pay, without complaint, and of course without thanks. He does not seem to realize that punctuality is not possible. We have people reporting for work who walked when the bus broke down, and he shouts at them as they limp in at the gate. Antonio is amazed that they come to work at all.

There are two men who waded a river to get to work when the floods washed the bridge away, and yet Heinz still wanted to dock their pay. Antonio refused to do this. He told Heinz: "Look, they have to **want to** come to work, to be appreciated here, or absenteeism will become far higher than it already is."

Heinz's story. Heinz explains that the factory was a real mess when he arrived. There was no order, no procedure, no discipline, and no responsibility.

He complains that Antonio is always making excuses. Everything is a special case or an exceptional circumstance. He runs around like a wet nurse trying to discover why the employees are unhappy or disturbed. He is forever telling Antonio to let them stand on their own two feet.

Employees think they can turn up to work when it is convenient for them, despite the fact that they know production cannot start until nearly all of them arrive. They wait for things to go wrong, and then act as if they are making heroic gestures of self-sacrifice. He has told them repeatedly that he does not need them to stay late, he just needs them to get to work on time.

They have more colorful excuses than a tale of the Wild West. To hear them tell it, they only come to work at all because they love us. And that they were late because their brothers missed an appointment, or some bridge fell down, or who knows what. We get "scenes of village life" here every day.

Heinz explains that he has told Antonio that he does not want to bully employees or harass them, he just wants to keep agreements, deadlines, and schedules. He does not believe that is too much to ask.

In this example, it should be noted, Heinz represents a very sophisticated Eiffel Tower culture, and Antonio quite an unsophisticated family one. In the hands of a sophisticated family culture, like many Japanese companies, the consequences could be different. Nor are cultures necessarily exclusive. Families can take on the exacting rules of Eiffel Towers and become formidable competitors. The finest combinations lie beyond stereotypes and simple contrasts.

THE GUIDED MISSILE CULTURE

The guided missile culture differs from both the family and the Eiffel Tower by being **egalitarian,** but differs also from the family and resembles the Eiffel Tower in being impersonal and task oriented. Indeed, the guided missile culture is rather like the Eiffel Tower in flight. But while the rationale of the Eiffel Tower culture is means, the guided missile has a rationale of ends. Everything must be done to persevere in your strategic intent and reach your target.

The guided missile culture is oriented to tasks, typically undertaken by teams or project groups. It differs from the role culture in that the jobs members do are not fixed in advance. They must do whatever it takes to complete a task, and what is needed is often unclear and may have to be discovered.

The National Aeronautics and Space Administration (NASA) pioneered the use of project groups working on space probes which resembled guided missiles. It takes roughly 140 different kinds of engineers to build a lunar landing module, and who's contribution is crucial at exactly what time cannot be known in advance. Because every variety of engineering must work harmoniously with every other, the best form of synthesis needs to be discovered in the course of working. Nor can there be any hierarchy which claims that "A's expertise is greater than B's expertise." Each knows most about his or her part. How the whole will function needs to be worked out with everyone's participation. All are **equals,** or at least potentially equal, since their relative contributions are not yet known.

Such groups will have leaders or coordinators who are responsible for sub- and final assemblies, but these generalists may know less than specialists in each discipline and must treat all experts with great respect. The group is egalitarian because it might need the help of any one expert in changing direction towards its target. The end is known, but the possible trajectories are uncertain.

Missile cultures frequently draw on professionals and are cross-disciplinary. In an advertising agency, for example, one copywriter, one visualizer/artist, one media buyer, one commercial film buyer, and one account representative may work on a campaign yet to be approved by the client. All will play a part, but what part depends on the final campaign the client prefers.

Guided missile cultures are expensive because professionals are expensive. Groups tend to be temporary relationships as fleeting as the project and largely instrumental in bringing the project to a conclusion. Employees will join other groups, for other purposes, within days or weeks, and may have multiple memberships. This culture is **not** affectionate or mutually committed, but typifies the **neutral** cultures discussed in Chapter 6.

The ultimate criteria of human value in the guided missile culture is how you perform and to what extent you contribute to the jointly desired outcome. In effect, each member shares in problem solving. The relative contribution of any one person may not be as clear as in the Eiffel Tower culture, where each role is described and outputs can be quantified.

In practice, the guided missile culture is **superimposed** upon the Eiffel Tower organization to give it permanence and stability. This is known as the matrix organization. You have one (Eiffel Tower) line reporting to your functional boss, say electrical engineering, and another (guided missile) line of responsibility to your project head. This makes you jointly responsible to your engineering boss for quality engineering and to your project leader for a viable, low-cost means of, say, auto emissions control. The project has to succeed, and your electronics must be excellent. Two authorities pull you in different, although reconcilable, directions.

Thinking, Learning, and Change

The guided missile culture is **cybernetic,** in the sense that it homes in on its target using feedback signals and is therefore circular rather than linear. Yet the missile rarely, if ever, changes its mind about its target. Steering is therefore corrective and conservative, not as open to new **ends** as to new **means.**

Learning includes getting along with people, breaking the ice quickly, playing the part in a team which is currently lacking, being practical rather than theoretical, and being problem centered rather than discipline centered. Appraisal is often by peers or subordinates rather than by someone up the hierarchy.

Change comes quickly to the guided missile culture. The target moves. More targets appear, new groups are formed, old ones dissolve. People who hop from group to group will often hop from job to job, so that turnover tends to be high, and **loyalties to professions and projects are greater than loyalties to the company.** The guided missile culture is, in many respects, the antithesis of the family culture, in which bonds are close and ties are of long duration and deep affection.

Motivating, Rewarding, and Resolving Conflict

Motivations tend to be **intrinsic** in this culture. That is, team members get enthusiastic about, identify with, and struggle towards the final product. In the case of the Macintosh Apple, the enthusiasm was about creating an "insanely great machine." The product under development is the superordinate goal for which the conflicts and animosities of team members may be set aside. Unless there is high participation, there will not be widespread commitment. The final consensus must be broad enough to pull in all those who worked on it.

This culture tends to be individualistic since it allows for a wide variety of differently specialized persons to work with each other on a temporary basis. The scenery of faces keeps changing. Only the pursuit of chosen lines of personal development is constant. The team is a vehicle for the shared enthusiasm of its members, but is itself disposable and will be discarded when the project ends. Members are garrulous, idiosyncratic, and intelligent, but their mutuality is a means, not an end. It is a way of enjoying the journey. They do not need to know each other intimately, and may avoid doing so. Management by objectives is the language spoken, and people are paid for performance.

THE INCUBATOR CULTURE

The incubator culture is based on the existential idea that organizations are secondary to the fulfillment of individuals. Just as "existence precedes essence" was the motto of existential philosophers, so "existence precedes organization" is the notion of incubator cultures.

If organizations are to be tolerated at all, they should be there to serve as **incubators for self-expression and self-fulfilment.** The metaphor here should not be confused with "business incubators." (These are organizations which provide routine maintenance and services, plant equipment, insurance, office space, and so on, for embryo businesses, so that they can lower their overhead costs during the crucial start-up phase.)

However, the logic of business and cultural incubators is quite similar. In both cases, the purpose is to free individuals from routine to more creative activities, and to minimize time spent on self-maintenance. The incubator is **both** personal and egalitarian. Indeed, it has almost no structure at all, and what structure it does provide is merely for personal convenience: heat, light, word processing, coffee, and so on.

The roles of other people in the incubator, however, are crucial. They are there to confirm, criticize, develop, find resources for, and help to complete the innovative product or service. The culture acts as a sounding board for innovative ideas and tries to respond intelligently to new initiatives. Typical examples are start-up firms in Silicon Valley, California, in Silicon Glen in Scotland, and on Route 128 around Boston. The companies are usually entrepreneurial or founded by a creative team that quit a larger employer just before the payoff. Being individualist, they are not constrained by organizational loyalties, and may deliberately "free ride" until their eggs are close to hatching. In this way, larger organizations find themselves successively undermined.

Cultural incubators are not only small innovative companies. They can be doctors in group practice, legal partners, some consultants, chartered surveyors, or any group of professionals who work mostly alone but like to share resources while comparing experiences. Some writers see the incubator as the organizational wave of the future. Others see the decline of Silicon Valley as evidence that this culture cannot survive maturity and is but a temporary phase in starting up an organization from an ad hoc basis. Others point to the rarity of incubator cultures outside the enclaves of individualism in America, the UK, and the English-speaking world.

Just as incubators have minimal structure, so they also have minimal hierarchy. Such authority as individuals do command is strictly personal, the exciting nature of their ideas and the inspiration of their vision leading others to work with them.

Incubators often, if not always, operate in an environment of intense **emotional** commitment. However, this commitment is less towards people per se than to the world-changing, society-redeeming nature of the work being undertaken. The personal computer will bring "power to the person," gene splicing could save crops, save lives, rescue the economy; they represent an odyssey into the unknown, wherein "the journey is the reward."

Incubator cultures enjoy the process of creating and innovating. Because of close relationships, shared enthusiasms, and superordinate goals, the incubator at its best can be ruthlessly honest, effective, nurturant, therapeutic, and exciting, depending as it does on face-to-face relationships and working intimacies. Because the association is voluntary, often underfunded and fueled largely by hope and idealism, it can be the most significant and intense experience of a lifetime. But this is very hard to repeat or sustain, since the project no sooner succeeds than strangers must be hired and the founders' special relationships are lost. Incubators are typically limited in size by the leaders' "span of control"; it becomes hard to communicate spontaneously and informally with more than 75–100 people.

Thinking, Learning, and Change

Change in the incubator can be fast and spontaneous where the members are attuned to each other. Roger Harrison[2] has likened the process to an improvising jazz band, where a self-elected leader tries something new and the band follows if it likes the theme and ignores the theme if it does not. All participants are on the same wavelength, empathically searching together for a solution to the shared problem. But because a customer has not defined any target, the **problem itself is open to redefinition,** and the solution being searched for is typically generic, aimed at a universe of applications.

American start-up companies with incubator cultures rarely survive the maturing of their products and their markets. This culture learns to create but not to **survive altered patterns of demand.** The great designers of the novel products continue to be the heroes of the company long after the focus has shifted to customer service and to marketing.

Motivating, Rewarding, and Resolving Conflict

Motivation is often wholehearted, intrinsic, and intense, with individuals working "70 hours a week and loving it," as the T-shirts at Apple Computer used to read in its earlier days. There is competition to contribute to the emerging shape of something new. Everyone wants to get his or her hands on. There is scant concern for personal security, and few wish to profit or have power **apart from the unfolding creative process.** If the whole succeeds, there will be plenty for everyone. If it does not, the incubator itself will be gone.

In contrast to the family culture, leadership in the incubator is **achieved,** not ascribed. You follow those whose progress most impresses you and whose ideas work. Power plays that impede group achievement will be reviled. Conflict is resolved either by splitting up or by trying the proposed alternatives to see which works best.

WHICH COUNTRIES PREFER WHICH CORPORATE CULTURES

As we have already said, these pure types seldom exist. In practice, the types are mixed or overlaid, with one culture dominating. Nevertheless, in different national cultures, one or more of these types clearly dominate the corporate scene, and if we list the main characteristics of the four types it becomes easy to refer back to the national cultural dimensions discussed in the preceding chapters. The following table (Figure 11–5, page 176) shows how, in the four models, employees relate differently, have different views of authority, think, learn, and change in different ways, and are motivated by different rewards, while criticism and conflict resolution are variously handled.

The original 79-item questionnaire used to compile our main database was not aimed at measuring the four corporate cultures, although it incidentally included the questions illuminating family and Eiffel Tower approaches described above (with results shown in Figures 11–2 through 11-4). Two years ago, however, the Centre for International Business Studies decided to start compiling a new database of corporate culture, using a similar approach.

FIGURE 11–5
Characteristics of the Four Corporate Cultures

	Family	Eiffel Tower	Guided Missile	Incubator
Relationships between employees	Diffuse relationships to organic whole to which one is bonded	Specific role in mechanical system of required interactions	Specific tasks in cybernetic system targeted upon shared objectives	Diffuse, spontaneous relationships growing out of shared creative process
Attitude towards authority	Status is ascribed to parent figures who are close and powerful	Status is ascribed to superior roles which are distant yet powerful	Status is achieved by project group members who contribute to targeted goal	Status is achieved by individuals exemplifying creativity and growth
Ways of thinking and learning	Intuitive, holistic, lateral, and error-correcting	Logical, analytical, vertical, and rationally efficient	Problem centered, professional, practical, cross-disciplinary	Process oriented, creative, ad hoc, inspirational
Attitudes towards people	Family members	Human resources	Specialists and experts	Co-creators
Ways of changing	"Father" changes course	Change rules and procedures	Shift aim as target moves	Improvise and attune
Ways of motivating and rewarding	Intrinsic satisfaction in being loved and respected	Promotion to greater position, larger role	Pay or credit for performance and problems solved	Participating in the process of creating new realities
	Management by subjectives	Management by job description	Management by objectives	Management by enthusiasm
Criticism and conflict resolution	Turn other cheek, save others' faces, do not lose power game	Criticism is accusation of irrationalism unless there are procedures to arbitrate conflicts	Constructive task-related only, then admit error and correct fast	Must improve creative idea, not negate it

Sixteen questions were devised which deal with general concepts of egalitarianism versus hierarchy, degrees of formality, different forms of conflict resolution, learning, and so on. (Examples of these are in Appendix 2.) Respondents are asked to choose between four possible descriptions of their company, which are geared respectively to the power-priority of the family, the role-dominance of the Eiffel Tower, the task-orientation of the guided missile, and the person-orientation of the incubator.

This work is fairly new; the database currently totals 3,000, and we only have significant samples for 12 countries. These, however, show very marked distinctions. Figure 11–6 (page 178) shows the results of totaling the responses to the whole questionnaire. This puts the highest scores for guided missile companies in America and the UK, and the highest for family companies in France and Spain. Sweden scores highest for incubators, and Germany for Eiffel Tower.

The reader, however, should interpret this cautiously. Smaller companies **wherever** located are more likely to take the family and incubator forms. Large companies needing structure to cohere are likely to choose Eiffel Tower or guided missile forms.

Our database has relatively few respondents from smaller companies, so that these are underrepresented. In France, for example, smaller companies tend to be family and larger companies Eiffel Tower. In America, guided missile companies may dominate among large corporations, but the archetypal incubators are to be found in Silicon Valley, as they are in the UK in Silicon Glen.

SUMMARY

We have defined four broad types of corporate culture, which are closely related to the national differences described in earlier chapters. Just as national cultures conflict, leading to mutual incomprehension and mistrust, so corporate cultures collide. Attempts to "dice" the family with a matrix can cause rage and consternation. Getting cozy with subordinates in the Eiffel Tower could be seen as a potentially improper advance. Asking to be put in a group with a special friend is a subversive act in the guided missile culture. Calling your boss "buddy" and slapping him or her on the back will get you thrown from the Eiffel Tower, while suggesting in an

FIGURE 11–6
National Patterns of Corporate Culture

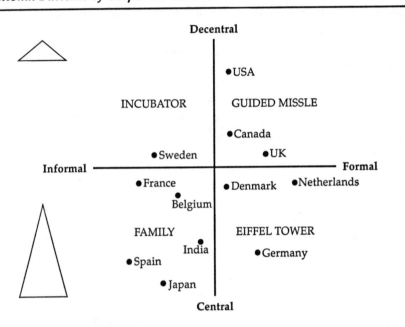

incubator that everyone fill out time-sheets will be greeted with cat-calls. (If you really want to discover norms, **break them;** reading this chapter is intended as a less painful alternative.)

Yet the types exist and must be respected. Really successful businesses borrow from all types and ceaselessly struggle to reconcile them. We turn to this process in the last chapter. First, however, we should say goodbye to Mr. Johnson.

Back in St. Louis at the MCC management meeting, Mr. Johnson reported on the introduction of pay-for-performance. It had been resisted widely, and where it had been tried, in parts of Southern Europe, the Middle East, and Asia, early results showed it had failed. The group listened in silence. The atmosphere was distinctly cool. "Well," said the CEO, "how do you plan to cope with these problems, Bill? I'm sure we don't need the human resources function to tell us that there are a lot of different people and opinions in the world."

Johnson had by now decided that he had nothing to lose, so he voiced a concern he had felt for many months. "I realize we make machines, but I sometimes ask myself if we are letting the metaphor run away with the organization. These are people, not microprocessors or integrated circuits which can be replaced if they don't work."

"I wish we **could** operate more like a computer," interrupted the finance manager. "We hire quality people to do as we tell them, and function in ways they are trained. Either they do this or we get somebody else. What's wrong with that?"

The CEO was trying to calm things down. "I have to disagree there," he said. "I see this company as more of an **organism**. If you go to Barcelona and chop off heads, don't be surprised if the body dies. If we take out some subsidiary's right hand, we can't expect it to work well in the future. What I can't understand is why Bill can't get them to see that we're all one organism, and that the hands and feet can't go off in all directions."

Suddenly all the exasperations of the last few months came to the surface. For a moment Johnson had thought that the CEO was supporting him, but it was the same old message: get the whole world to march in step with us.

"What **I've** been through in the last eight months is about as far from a smoothly running computer or a living organism as you could get. I'll tell you what it's really like, because I was reading the story to my kids. It's like that crazy croquet game in *Alice in Wonderland* where she has to play with a flamingo as a mallet, waiters bending over as hoops, and hedgehogs as balls. The flamingo twists its head round to look at Alice, the hoops wander off, and the balls crawl away. The result is chaos.

"Other cultures aren't part of a machine, nor the organs of a supranational body. They're different animals, all with logic of their own. If we asked them what game **they** are playing, and got them to explain the rules, we might discover when we aren't holding a mallet at all, or even get the hedgehog to go in the right direction."

Was Mr. Johnson promoted, or given the job of overseeing the welfare of MCC pensioners? My guess is that he is running a small but fast-growing consultancy somewhere, specializing in cross-cultural management.

REFERENCES

1. Inzerilli, G., and A. Laurent, *The Concept of Organizational Structure*, Working Paper, University of Pennsylvania and INSEAD, 1979; "Managerial Views of Organizational Structure in France and the USA," *International Studies of Management and Organizations*, XIII, 1–2, 1983, pp. 97–118.
2. Harrison, R., "Understanding Your Organization's Character," *Harvard Business Review*, May–June 1972.

General

Hampden-Turner, C., *Corporate Culture*, The Economist Books/Business Books, London, 1991.

Handy, C., *The Gods of Management*, Souvenir Press, London, 1978.

Chapter Twelve

Towards International and Transnational Management

This book has elucidated national differences, of which we have found a great many. So wide and pervasive are these variations that they would seem to confirm the doubt expressed at the beginning as to whether universal or general principles of how to manage were feasible or useful.

Yet the implication of the research presented here is that universals exist at another level. While you cannot give universal **advice** that will work regardless of culture, and while general axioms of business administration turn out to be largely American cultural axioms, there are **universal dilemmas or problems of human existence.** Every country and every organization in that country faces dilemmas:

- In relationships with people
- In relationship to time
- In relations between people and the natural environment

While nations differ markedly in **how** they approach these dilemmas, they do not differ in needing to make some kind of response. People everywhere are as one in having to face up to the same challenges of existence.

In this last chapter we look at some of the specific problems faced by international management, arising under the headings of structure, strategy, communications, and human resources, and consider a common approach to their solution.

My research methodology consists of stories, scenes, situations, and questions which put two moral and/or managerial principles in conflict. It is the researchers who force the managers to prefer one over the other. In reality, each of the managers whose reactions have gone to make up the database was explaining which was his or her first and which his or her second foundation stone in **building the moral edifice.**

Some felt that you had to give priority to a universal rule (universalism) and behave in particular instances accordingly. Some felt that you have to give priority to your affection for particular people (particularism) and develop whatever universals you could out of such obligations. But few were actually rejecting the alternative solution out of hand, and, as the figures show, it is rare for any national result to be anywhere near 100 percent in favor of any priority. Almost all our problems, and their solutions, are recognizable all over the world.

There is another important respect in which all the world's managers are the same. Whichever principle they start with, the circumstances of business and of organizing experience require them to reconcile the dilemmas we have been discussing. You can only prosper if as many particulars as possible are covered by rules, yet exceptions are seen and noted. You can only think effectively if both the specifics and the diffuse wholes, the segments and the integrations, are covered. Whether you are at heart an individualist or a collectivist, your individuals must be capable of organizing themselves, and your collectives are only as good as the health, wealth, and wisdom of each member.

It is crucial to give status to achievers, but equally crucial to back strategies, projects, and new initiatives from people who have not yet achieved anything, in other words to ascribe status to these in hope of facilitating success. Everyone should be equal in their rights and opportunities, yet any contest will produce a hierarchy of relative standings.

Respect for age and experience can both nurture and discourage the young and inexperienced. Hierarchy and equality are finely interwoven in every culture. It is true that time is both a passing sequence of events and a moment of truth, a "now" in which past, present, and future are given new meanings.

We need to accept influences from the depth of our inner convictions and the world around us. In the final analysis, **culture is the manner in which these dilemmas are reconciled, since every nation seeks a different and winding path to its own ideals of integrity.** It is my position that businesses will succeed to the extent that this reconciliation occurs, so we have everything to learn from discovering how others have traveled to their own positions.

PROBLEMS FOR THE CROSS-CULTURAL MANAGER

I am not the first to note these differences. Geert Hofstede did so in his international samples of IBM executives,[1] as did Inzerilli and Laurent[2] in their research comparing Italian and French managers to those in America, Japan, and Europe. As we tracked the experience of Mr. Johnson of MCC from chapter to chapter, we found what these researchers have also noted, that favorite American solutions do not always solve the dilemmas of other nations. Since America has been the principal source of management theory, this is crucial information for all students of business practice.

For example, the matrix organization is a very clever reconciliation of the need to be organized by discipline and function and the need to respond to projects, products under development, and customer specifications. But while this solves American, British, Dutch, and Scandinavian dilemmas, it directly threatens and contradicts the family model described in Chapter 11, so that some Italian, Spanish, French, and Asian companies will have to devise a different solution.

Similarly, Peter Drucker's management by objectives is a justly famous reconciliation of an American dilemma which has rightly been adopted by like-minded nations. The conflict between equality and hierarchy and the individual and the collective is reconciled by getting individuals to pledge themselves freely to fulfill the key objectives of the collective and the hierarchy. Voluntarily negotiated contracts join the person to the group. That is good, but not so good for nations which regard the performance of individuals as part of the relationship with the boss, and who attribute excellence to the whole family or relationship.

Pay-for-performance is similarly an attempted solution to the achievement–ascription dilemma. Why not ascribe status and financial rewards to employees in proportion to their achievements? Again, this has great appeal to those who put achievement first, but none to those who put ascription first and seek to be the emotional "authors" of a subordinate's success. We discussed this problem in detail in Chapter 8, but it is so central to the issue that it will bear an additional anecdote here.

An American computer company introduced pay-for-performance in both America and the Middle East. It worked well in America, and increased sales briefly in the Middle East before a serious slump occurred. Inquiries showed that indeed the winners among salesmen in the Middle East had done better, but the vast majority had done worse. The wish for their fellows to succeed had been seriously eroded by the contest. Overall morale and sales were down. Ill will was contagious. When the bosses discovered that certain salesmen were earning more than they did, high individual performances also ceased. But the principal reason for eventually abandoning the system was the discovery that customers were being loaded up with products they could not sell. As A tried to beat B to the bonus, the care of customers began to slip, with serious, if delayed, results.

Centralization versus Decentralization

The main dilemma which those who manage across cultures confront is the extent to which they should **centralize,** thereby imposing on foreign cultures rules and procedures that might affront them, or **decentralize,** thereby letting each culture go its own way, without having any centrally viable ideas about improvement since the "better way" is a local, not a global pathway. If you radically decentralize, you have to ask whether the headquarters can add value at all, or whether companies acting in several nations are worthwhile.

Decentralization is easier under some corporate cultures than others. To decentralize, you have to delegate. Of the four models described in Chapter 11, this can be done in the Eiffel Tower and the guided missile cultures, but not so easily in the family model where the parent remains the parent. Stories are common of the difficulties that Japanese managers have in decentralizing and delegating to foreigners. The family communicates by a kind of in-house osmosis of empathy and bowing rituals that foreigners cannot easily share. Policies are made on the telephone lines to Tokyo because the intimate understandings between Japanese insiders are very difficult to delegate.

As most of our case histories and anecdotes have shown, mis-communication is far more common than dialogue. Nevertheless, centralizing and decentralizing are, like all the other dimensions introduced in this book, potentially reconcilable processes. A biological organism grows to higher levels of order and complexity by being more differentiated and more integrated. The more departments, divisions, functions, and differentiated activities a corporation pursues, the greater the challenge, and also the greater the importance of **coordinating all this variety.**

As Paul Lawrence and Jay Lorsch[3] showed in the late 1960s, both over-centralized (over-integrated) and over-decentralized (over-differentiated) companies underperform to significant degrees. Differentiating and integrating need to be synergized or reconciled. The corporation with the best-integrated diversity is the one which excels.

Group management is often fooled by a foreign subsidiary doing as it is asked by headquarters, but essentially performing a corporate rain dance. The local managers know it will make no difference to the rainfall, but if headquarters wants a list of everyone's qualifications and salaries to compare the two, they will provide one. Never mind that the qualifications have probably been invented to fit the existing salaries. When these perfect scores arrive, headquarters feels it is in control worldwide, but of course this is an illusion. The policy handbook says "we pay no bribes," but, in many countries, paid they will be. Relationships without presents are impossible.

The centralizing–decentralizing dilemma is often experienced as consistency versus flexibility of corporate identity. Is it more important for Shell to relate successfully in the Philippines by helping peasants to raise pigs, or should the strategy of being an energy company be used to maintain continuity? In practice, the pig farming has helped to prevent oil pipelines being blown up by communist insurgents. If you are digging for oil in Nigeria, why not find some water, too, and build some desperately needed wells?

Examples of this kind show that the relationship between centralization and decentralization is a subtle one. It is not true that every differentiated activity takes you further from your core business simply because it is different. Water wells and pig farms may make all the difference between gaining business in less developed countries or losing it. It is **because we are all different that we have so much to exchange with each other.** In matters of culture, as in the relationship of the sexes, the difference can be the chief source of attraction. Italian design and Dutch engineering can lead to conflicts, as we have seen; they could also lead to a product made in heaven.

The ideal, then, is to differentiate in such a way as to make integration more effective, or to decentralize activities in such a way that an ever broader diversity gets coordinated by the "central nervous system" of your corporation. In matters of cultural diversity, there is always a challenge, but, where this challenge is met, valuable connections result.

Quality, not Quantity, in Decentralization

It is not a matter of **how much** to decentralize, but **what** to decentralize and what to keep at corporate headquarters. A company that does not centralize information cannot cohere at all, but this does not mean that decisions cannot be made locally. Arguably technical specifications, for example, the rules, standards, and procedures by which oil refineries are operated, can be decided centrally, but what mix of products to refine could be decided nationally, close to customers' changing demands.

Pricing may also be a local decision, sensitive to the proximity of competitors and the degree of overcapacity. Financing decisions are normally allocated centrally or locally according to their size. National companies often pay a standard overhead to headquarters, and get legal, financial, planning, and personnel services "free"; this arrangement tends to protect the role of centralized functions. You have to pay, so you might as well use them. Alternatively, headquarters staff may provide consultancy services to national companies on request. Under this system, unnecessary staff services at headquarters will shrivel on the vine if no one wants them, an argument which tends to favor decentralization.

INTERNATIONAL AND TRANSNATIONAL COMPANIES

The issues of centralization and decentralization have been fully discussed by Christopher Bartlett and Sumantra Ghoshal in relation to their analysis of global-versus-multinational and international-versus-transnational corporations.[4]

As they define them, global and multinational companies are both essentially centralized, in that their subsidiaries relate to the head company or country, even if not necessarily very strongly, rather than to the other companies or nations in the group. For these companies, there are unlikely to be many foreigners in the top management team, and the myth of the universal applicability of management techniques is likely to be strong.

In contrast, in both international and transnational corporate structures, there is a significant attempt to overcome the dilemma of centralization versus decentralization; each of these in its own way sets out to manage diversity and gain competitive advantage from being located in different countries with special capacities. This book is aimed at those who are already operating on international or transnational levels, or aspire to do so.

The two forms take different paths to the reconciliation of centralizing and decentralizing. The international corporation moves out influence from its center to regions and nations, retaining a coordinative role, while the transnational corporation loses its center in favor of polycentric influences from different parts of its network.

The **international** corporation, of which Shell, ABB, Ericsson, and Procter & Gamble are examples, breaks with the notion that national organizations are spokes around a wheel. National organizations have legitimate relationships with each other based on what it is that the customer wants and the best source of supply within the international system. The headquarter's role becomes not so much to instruct or to evaluate as to **co-ordinate,** to make sure that if one nation has embarked in a promising direction, other nations also learn from this. Headquarters facilitates this, and possibly helps other nations to emulate the initiative.

International corporations are likely to have top management teams which are a microcosm of the whole system, with Germans, Dutch, French, Italian, and Japanese executives at company headquarters where considerable businesses are located in those countries. These are not delegates or representatives in a foreign country, but full-time contributors to multi-cultural management, so that, say, the Italian subsidiary has its cultural traits not only within but at the coordinating center.

As corporations move from a multi-local to an international form, the headquarters behaves **less like a policeman and more like a**

consultant. Hence the Shell International Petroleum Company speaks not of a headquarters but of central offices (divided between London and the Hague). It has no CEO or controlling center, but a committee of managing directors, each with local responsibilities in addition to central ones. Functional and geographical chiefs are called coordinators, their authority stemming from the fact that they know what several functions, regions, or nations are doing.

The **transnational** corporation is polycentric rather than coordinated from the center. It consists of several centers of specialized excellence which will exercise authority and influence whenever these are qualified to do so by the challenge confronting the organization. Gunnar Hedlund, a Swedish professor, sees this as increasingly typical of some Swedish organizations such as IKEA and Ericsson, for example. Bartlett and Ghoshal regard transnationalism as an important future direction, rather than a reality, in which companies such as Philips and Matsushita are heading. Jay Ogilvy, an American academic, has spoken of heterarchies replacing hierarchies.[5]

All these predictions of the future form of the successful transnational imply a flatter corporate structure drawing on a multiplicity of points of expertise. Hence, if a company was designing a new international sports car, the electronics might come from Japan, the engine and suspension from Germany, the design from Italy, the fiberglass shell from the Netherlands, the mahogany wood finish from Britain, and the assembly might be done in Spain. National marketing departments will adopt different tactics to sell it, while exchanging experience and drawing upon each other's brand management expertise. Each element in the value-added chain or loop would exercise authority on the issue of its own cultural strength.

Robert Reich, US Secretary of Labor, has argued[6] that it does not really matter any more who owns the company, be they American shareholders, Europeans, or Asians. What matters is where the greatest value is added in the transnational network. Countries will prosper or stagnate by the skills they inject into these value chains. In the economy of the future, knowledge is king, and influence flows from wherever that knowledge resides.

In the transnational company, influence can be exercised by any nation on one or more others and can start at any point, accumulating value as it goes and circling to reconcile cultural strengths.

What is important about transnationalism is that it follows the circular reconciliations sketched at the ends of Chapters 3–10.

You can join Italy's particularism to Germany's universalism, or join American individualism and inner-directed creativity to Japanese rapid collectivist exploitation of new products and other-directed skills of customer satisfaction. Where countries specialize in what they do best, the transnational circuits so formed could prove unbeatable. The remaining question is how the transnational organization is to survive the complete atrophy of its center.

HUMAN RESOURCE MANAGEMENT IN THE FUTURE

The main preoccupation of our analysis of cultural differences has been under the general heading of human resources. In the recruitment of the senior managers of the future, large companies seem at present (recession apart) to be at some disadvantage. The notion that it is desirable to gain power by climbing high in large organizations is currently somewhat out of fashion; autonomy is more sought after, especially, it would seem, in Northwestern Europe, and the attraction to recruits of internationalism is more likely to lie in the experience, knowledge, and investigation of multiple cultures.

Recruits will want to plan their own careers in the international and transnational corporation of the future, and some career ladders may look more like "walkabouts." Companies which succeed in reconciling the centralization versus decentralization dilemma will have learned how to rotate their employees internationally (especially the high flyers), how to work in several languages, and how to make decisions at many points on the globe and to spread their effects.

Once the scarce commodity of intelligent managers has been attracted, the future transnational will set out to give them further training in cross-cultural awareness, starting with learning how to recognize a cultural problem, which, as we have seen, is often unidentified; it is not a problem, but "the stubbornness of South Europeans about incentive schemes." People who resist American universals are seen as traditional, unbusinesslike, or even backward.

THE GROWTH OF INFORMATION

I once gave a seminar in Thailand that saved a company $1.5 million. It was not, alas, the result of any insights I imparted. A French executive sitting next to a Thai executive of the same company discovered that the latter was about to build a pilot plant which would duplicate something the French had just completed. This is indicative of the frequent failure of internal corporate communications.

The development of information technology (IT), however, presents new problems. IT has its own curious forms of absolutism. Given the high capacity, high speed, and high cost of computers, the impulse following their installation is to generate a great deal of information as quickly as possible, thereby reducing the cost-per-byte.

To know everything statistical about your subsidiary before it has even discovered this itself is therefore much prized. I have heard of subsidiary companies called up during breakfast (because of time zone differences) with complaints that tin wastage rates in the canning plants are up 50 percent.

This approach can have disastrous consequences for intercultural communication, and militates against the development of international or transnational structures. The head of a national subsidiary is paid in part to use his or her discretion, free of oversight. If you seek a genuine cultural contribution from a foreign subsidiary, you cannot check up on it daily. Information should go first and foremost to those whose operations it concerns, with a lag before headquarters gets it. This gives time for local answers to be found and actions to be taken.

A company will remain a centralized, directive, global organization so long as information is used for power and advantage. Because information depends on input, it is easily distorted. Subsidiaries punished for not meeting their forecasts will lower the forecast next time. IT can give an illusion of control which does not survive closer examination.

In the international and transnational structures, national operating companies communicate because they wish to, and because the parallel activities of other companies in nearby markets are opportunities and resources. The IT philosophy in these structures states that every national company is free to take major initiatives without prior consultation, but should keep the network informed of its actions. It has local autonomy, but no right to secrecy about the exercise of that autonomy after the fact. All interested parties must know what has been done.

A good software for keeping networks informed is the highlight system. Any interested subsidiary or centralized function can tap into those activities which concern it. This allows for ad hoc project groups to take advantage of any number of converging lines of research or activity. The hallmark of the international or transnational structure is lateral connections between activities capable of being catalyzed to the advantage of the whole network. Recall that, in this structure, subsidiaries connect to subsidiaries. Like hounds hunting for a fox, anyone may pick up the scent, bay loudly, and have the others follow the new direction.

Software, moreover, may be more or less culturally compatible with how managers think. Diffuse ways of thinking and learning are often diagrammatic and configurative. Streams of words are more linear, specific, and sequential. "Windows" allow for selective viewing of information by those interested.

The shape of software needs to be a microcosm of the larger structure and consistent with it. There is software for scenarios of alternative futures, for creative connections between ideas, for alternative applications of key technologies, and for spin-offs. There will in the future be software to facilitate cross-cultural communication by comparing your individual responses to dilemmas with those of another culture.[7]

IMPLICATIONS FOR BUSINESS STRATEGY

Culture can all too easily put brakes on any movement to internationalize. Universalism tends to create global structures in which the values of the home country are celebrated worldwide. Individualism can produce multinational structures in deference to the individuality of each nation. Inner-directedness also contributes to global or multinational structures, depending on whether the inner-direction is towards a parent company (a global structure) or a national group (a multinational structure).

Equality, other-directedness, and achievement orientations will encourage internationalization, and it is notable that both the Dutch and the Swedes, who display these attributes, are quite successful internationally. Family-style corporate cultures may work well in their countries of origin, but be difficult to transfer overseas. Eiffel Tower cultures will be rejected in nations with family-style traditions, especially if the "universals" are foreign. Guided missile cultures also offend family feeling with their on-again, off-again relationships and their "two fathers."

The principal implication for business strategy is a healthy respect for the founding beliefs of foreign cultures and the images they have chosen to create coherence. A "strange" culture usually has values neglected in ours, and to discover these is to find lost parts of our own cultural heritage. Hence, family-style cultures can remind us that work is not necessarily alienating, impersonal, and self-seeking. We can benefit from such insights without putting our relatives on the payroll or feeling like children when the boss walks in. International and transnational structures allow us to **synthesize the advantages of all cultures while avoiding their excesses.** Families are quite capable of nurturing independence and encouraging achievement. Managing across cultures gives you more possible pathways to your goal.

The only strategic system open to a genuinely international company will be the system described by Michael Goold[8] as **strategic control.** Here, strategy is neither laid down by the center nor subject to strict financial parameters, but fed to the center by national companies. They propose and the center co-ordinates, criticizes, approves, and adds its own funds. What occurs is a multi-cultural negotiation.

An international or transnational structure greatly reduces its own powers unless it gives a free to certain national, cultural proclivities. Strategies tend to vary with national culture; hence, inner-directed, universalistic, specific, achievement-oriented cultures, typically the English-speaking ones, talk as if they were engaged in military campaigns, saturating consumers with a withering hail of commercials and generally conquering and occupying markets.

In contrast, outer-directed, particularistic, diffuse, and ascription-oriented cultures, typically the Japanese and the "four little dragons," speak as if they were serenading customers before climbing into bed with them. They do not use the word "strategy" at all, although they clearly have a method of co-evolving with customers.

Individualist cultures with a sequential view of time, like America and Britain, are usually short-term in their business strategies. Collectivist cultures with a synchronous view of time, like Germany and Japan, are typically long-term strategically.

An international or transnational structure which does not allow those willing to postpone rewards for several years to do so could miss out on the secret of Asian and German economic strengths. Within the international or transnational structure, a microcosm of international economic competition is going on. We would be foolish not to notice who is winning or why, and to fail to apply the lessons.

LOCAL FREEDOM TO PRIORITIZE EMPLOYMENT VALUES

One interesting way of combining the universal values generated by the head office with local flexibility and the impact of national cultures arises in assessment procedures. The head office makes a list of what is to be appraised, but leaves their priorities to the national operating company. Shell, for example, until recently operated its HAIRL system of basic appraisal. HAIRL stands for Helicopter (the capacity to take a broad view from above), power of Analysis, Imagination, sense of Reality, and Leadership effectiveness. We were interested to discover if these were equally important to various Shell operating companies, and asked participants in several seminars to prioritize HAIRL for themselves. The results were as follows.

Netherlands	France	Germany	Britain
Reality	Imagination	Leadership	Helicopter
Analysis	Analysis	Analysis	Imagination
Helicopter	Leadership	Reality	Reality
Leadership	Helicopter	Imagination	Analysis
Imagination	Reality	Helicopter	Leadership

There is no inherent reason, it seems to me, why all nations should place equal weight on all values. If the Dutch want to stress realism, so be it. They find most of the oil by drilling where it really is, and not where they imagine it to be. Prioritizing the values of assessment can tell us a lot about how cultures vary.

It is the theme of this book that all cultures need to be both universalist and particularist, both individual and collective, both ascriptive and achieving, both inner- and outer-directed. Their difference lies in their priorities, where they "start." I have argued the essential **complementarity** of values. To post an individualist to collectivized Singapore can help to make that collectivism more responsive to individuals, and the reverse would be true of posting a Singaporean to America.

We should not forget that different priorities are not all equally successful. From studying different value priorities in different cultures come vital clues as to how we can better manage our own affairs.

LOCAL FREEDOM TO REWARD

It is similarly possible to have a universal rule that "success must be rewarded commensurate with its size," yet leave the form of that reward up to the national company. Our case study of MCC conveyed that message. That company was unable to accept that, while it could have a central philosophy of pay-for-performance, it needed to decentralize its application. Managers around the world are in favor of the principle; the difficulty is that they all mean different things by pay and different things by performance.

It is entirely reasonable that a person in a collectivist culture should seek to reward the team members for his or her own successful efforts. They get the money he helped generate; he gets the respect, affection, and gratitude, which is not such a bad bargain. That the high performer in an individualistic society might like to attract rewards away from colleagues is also entirely reasonable.

The solution is for collectivist and individualist cultures to give group rewards and personal rewards in accordance with their own judgments and results. After all, no culture pays salaries entirely as bonus for individual effort; part is always fixed, so we are talking about relative emphasis. In a truly international or transnational corporation, **every nation would be charged with finding its optimal mix between personal and group rewards,** with more of that reward for successful operations.

If we do this, we might be surprised. Do individuals in Western cultures create because of extrinsic rewards like money, or because their peers encourage them? The answers could be instructive.

Hierarchical versus egalitarian pay structures could also be up to the national company. Relatively equal pay may improve cooperation. Relatively unequal pay may increase competition among employees. How much of each works best? The company should have a fixed ratio of its turnover to distribute as it sees fit.

National companies might also be given the discretion to take lower salaries overall so as to reduce prices to customers, using a strategy of increasing market share. The notion that everyone is motivated principally by money rewards needs to be challenged. Those willing to take long-term advantage of wage control strategies should be encouraged. Corporate cultures based on the image of the family may not care so much about wage levels. Those who work principally for each other's affection can be fiercely competitive on costs, as the Japanese have shown. Pay-for-performance tends to be expensive.

Especially when people are poor, a group or collective orientation may be crucial for takeoff. A group bonus scheme used by Shell Nigeria, for example, was a water well and irrigation scheme for the town the employees lived in, which materially benefited their homes and neighborhood besides raising their status in the community. Arguably, such a scheme was far more valuable to individual employees than dividing the cost of the project between them and giving them the money instead.

THE ERROR-CORRECTING MANAGER

Other cultures are strange, ambiguous, even shocking to us. It is unavoidable that we will make mistakes in dealing with them, and feel muddled and confused. The real issue is how quickly we are prepared to learn from mistakes, and how bravely we struggle to understand a game in which perfect scores are an illusion, and where reconciliation only comes after a difficult passage through alien territory.

We need a certain amount of humility and a sense of humor to discover cultures other than our own, a readiness to enter a room in the dark and stumble over unfamiliar furniture until the pain in our shins reminds us where things are. World culture is a myriad of different ways of creating the integrity without which life and business cannot be conducted. There are no universal answers, but there are universal questions or dilemmas, and that is where we all need to start.

REFERENCES

1. Hofstede, G., *Culture's Consequences*, Sage, London, 1980.
2. Inzerilli, G., and A. Laurent, "Managerial Views of Organization Structure in France and the USA," *International Studies of Management and Organizations*, XIII, 1–2, 1983.
3. Lawrence, P. R., and J. W. Lorsch, *Organization and Environment: Managing Differentiation and Integration*, Irwin, Homewood, Illinois, 1967.
4. Bartlett, C., and S. Ghoshal, *Managing Across Borders*, Hutchinson Business Books, London, 1990.
5. Ogilvy, J., *Global Business Network*, Ameryville, California (personal communication).
6. Reich, R. B., *The Work of Nations: Preparing Ourselves for the 21st Century*, Knopf, 1991.
7. Under development by the Centre for International Business Studies, Amstelveen, Netherlands.
8. Goold, M., *Strategic Control*, The Economist Books/Business Books, London, 1990.

Appendix One

Some Technical Aspects of the Trompenaars Data Bank

Peter B. Smith
University of Sussex

The primary purpose of the Trompenaars data bank is to cast light upon differences between managerial subcultures to be found across different national cultures. In evaluating its strengths and weaknesses, it is therefore important to make analyses at the level of national cultures, rather than to focus on individual variations within each cultural group. This approach has both advantages and disadvantages. The principal advantage is that the averaging of individual responses should give the best estimate of each population mean. The disadvantage is that country means can never be relied upon to tell us the values or orientation of any one individual within that country.

The accuracy of the estimates of the average characteristics of managers in a given national culture will depend on many factors including sample size, the homogeneity of the culture, the breadth of sampling, the relevance and meaning of the questions posed, and so forth. The comments which follow are restricted to the 47 national cultures from which 50 or more responses are currently available. The present database of 14,993 responses includes two countries with over 1,000 responses (Britain and the Netherlands), 35 with over 100 responses, and 10 with 50–100 responses.

The regional distribution is as follows.

North America	5.0%
South America	4.7%
Europe	57.3%
Africa	4.5%
Australia/New Zealand	1.8%
Asia	7.0%
Others (incl. Middle East, Caribbean)	19.6%

Six of the Trompenaars scales are constructed from a series of items, each of which is said to represent the dimension to be measured. Their reliability may therefore be estimated by Cronbach's alpha.

Figure A1–1 shows the reliability of each of these scales. The remaining scale, time orientation, does not comprise a series of free-standing items and cannot be evaluated in this way.

After some comment on the time needed for completing the original 79-item questionnaire, a 58-item version was developed. This kept the most reliable items, and produced new scales for the less reliable items. Some items were recombined (25 questions were addressed to items that were not part of the scales but were closely related to the underlying concepts). The reliability coefficients of the 58-item questionnaire are shown in the right hand column, as well as the number of questions used. The number of new items is indicated by an asterisk (*).

These figures indicate that the reliability of the scales ranges from moderate to excellent. On the 79-item basis, the value for individualism–collectivism is below that usually thought acceptable, a finding which is consistent with the difficulty other researchers have found in scaling it reliably. On the 58-item basis, the INCO scale has been adapted from six to five items, two of which are new. The reliability factors did increase, and its face validity got much higher.

A second question to ask of the data bank is how the dimensions relate to one another. Figure A1–2 (page 200)shows that there are a number of significant linkages between several of the dimensions.

The fact that some of these correlations are quite substantial does not necessarily imply that separating out the different dimensions

FIGURE A1–1
Cronbach Alpha Reliabilities

	79-Item	58-Item
Universalism–particularism (UNPA)	0.75 (4)	0.76 (3)
Individualism–collectivism (INCO)	0.52 (6)	0.72 (5,2*)
Affective neutral–affectivity (ANAF)	0.64 (5)	0.63 (3,3*)
Specificity–diffuseness (SPDI)	0.61 (5)	0.61 (6,4*)
Achievement–ascription (ACHASC)	0.77 (6)	0.78 (4,1*)
Internality–externality (INTEX)	0.86 (28)	0.77 (10)

*See text on page 198.

is unnecessary. Significant country-level correlations between, for instance, universalism and achieved status indicate only that both orientations are high in a particular national culture, and not that they are necessarily endorsed by the same individuals or within the same organizations.

A third check on the representativeness of the country means on each dimension can be achieved through reference to the demographic profile of each country's respondents. Data is available on age, sex (65 percent of the database is male and 35 percent female), education, type of industry, present job, and religious affiliation. The largest management job category is manufacturing (over 1,500), followed by marketing and personnel, each with approximately 1,200 respondents. Analyses of co-variance can be used to adjust the country means in accordance with differences in demographic profile. When this is done, it is found that only modest changes in means occur. The rank orders reported earlier in this book remain substantially similar.

Each of the analyses reported above addresses the matter of how reliable are the country means. A second issue of importance concerns their predictive validity. It is not possible to assess this on the basis of data within the data bank. The principal bases upon which validity could be more firmly established would be formulation of hypotheses as to economic performance achieved within different national cultures, and as to types of misunderstandings and miscommunications likely to occur frequently between members of different national cultures.

FIGURE A1–2
Correlations between Dimensions

	UNPA	INCO	SPDI	ANAF	INTEX	ACHASC
TIMEOR	.00	−0.26	0.26	−0.25	−0.16	0.17
UNPA		0.43[a]	0.25	0.28	0.36[b]	0.47
INCO			0.06	0.21	0.17	0.29[b]
SPDI				−0.35[b]	−0.09	0.24
ANAF					0.24	−0.05
INTEX						0.53[a]

N = 47.

[a] P<0.01.

[b] p<0.05

Appendix Two

Examples from the 16 Questions Used to Measure Corporate Culture

Question 9: Criticism

In your organization, criticism:

a. Is aimed at the task, not the person
b. Is only given when asked for
c. Is mostly negative and usually takes the form of blame
d. Is avoided because people are afraid of hurting each other

Question 11: Conflict

In your organization, conflict:

a. Is controlled by the intervention of higher authority, and often fostered by it to maintain power
b. Is suppressed by reference to rules, procedures, and definitions of responsibility
c. Is resolved through full discussion of the merits of the work issues involved
d. Is resolved by open and deep discussion of personal needs and the values involved

Question 13: Hierarchy

In your organization, hierarchies:

a. Are redundant because each person is working for his or her own professional development

b. Are necessary because people have to know who has authority over whom

c. Are determined by the power and authority of the people involved

d. Are relevant only if they are useful for getting the task done

Responses

The possible responses relate as follows to company models:

Question 9:

a. Guided missile
b. Family
c. Incubator
d. Eiffel Tower

Question 11:

a. Family
b. Eiffel Tower
c. Guided missile
d. Incubator

Question 13:

a. Incubator
b. Family
c. Eiffel Tower
d. Guided missile

Appendix Three

Centre for International Business Studies

The Centre for International Business Studies (CIBS), of which Fons Trompenaars is managing director, is an internationally operating consulting firm with wide experience. It helps companies address the problems and challenges of intercultural management. CIBS concentrates above all on consulting with the managements of organizations on how to cope with differences between management practices in various cultures. In addition, CIBS offers business briefings, seminars, workshops, and specialized business topics in the following areas:

- Cultural awareness
- Negotiating skills across cultures
- Managing across cultures
- Intercultural communication and teamwork
- Country and regional briefings (for instance, working in The Netherlands and other European countries)
- Getting to grips with Japan
- Organizational culture and effectiveness
- Managing interdepartmental relationships
- Cultural aspects within mergers and acquisitions

For more information contact CIBS at:

Laan van Kronenburg 14
1183 AS Amstelveen
The Netherlands

tel 31 (0)20-640 33 11
fax 31 (0)20-640 31 51

Reviews

"The concepts he (Fons) uses are not only stimulating in themselves and provide fascinating insights into the subject of culture, but are also supported by vivid and practical examples."

Ken McKinlay, *Personnel Director, ICI Pharmaceuticals*

"I heartily recommend *Riding the Waves of Culture* for its broad-based data approach, its keen insights, and Fons's inimitable humor."

Kay R. Whitmore, *Chairman and Chief Executive, Eastman Kodak*

"Reinforces the importance of understanding cultural diversity in business in a way that is clear, powerful, and compelling."

Mort Topfer, *Executive Vice President, Motorola Inc.*

"A very welcome addition to the literature for business leaders wishing to internationalize their business."

Jaap Leemhuis, *Strategy Manager for Far East, Australasia, Manufacturing, Shell International Petroleum Mj BV*

"*Riding the Waves of Culture* offers an insightful and practical tool for understanding a complex, sometimes sensitive, topic. Leaders of global organizations should find it very useful in understanding and managing cultural similarities and differences."

Edsel D. Dunford, *President & Chief Operating Officer, TRW Inc.*

"At last . . . a clear, concise, readable explanation of the critical cultural dimensions of international management."

David C. Wigglesworth, PhD, *International/Cultural Management Professional and President, D.C.W. Associates International*

"Fons Trompenaars makes use of a simple and creative model; the fundamental beliefs in the center, which every culture hides under layers and reveals one by one—values and norms, manifestations and behavior. What the author strives to accomplish—making the reader understand the general structure of cultures—he succeeded at perfectly.

"The great contribution of Mr. Trompenaars is to make the reader understand the variety of cultures. While there is 'my' culture, and cultures of others, all cultures help people to solve their own problems.

Diversity isn't the opposite of problem solving, it is complementary. This is why I like this book."

Jacques Casanova, *Senior Vice President,*
Human Resources, Elf Aquitaine Group

INDEX

Other books of interest to you from Irwin Professional Publishing . . .

A MANAGER'S GUIDE TO GLOBALIZATION

SIX KEYS TO SUCCESS IN A CHANGING WORLD

Stephen H. Rhinesmith

Co-published with the American Society for Training and Development
Helps your organization develop a flexible, responsive corporate culture and adapt to today's dynamic international market. (240 pages)
ISBN: 1–55623–904–1

GLOBAL TRAINING

HOW TO DESIGN A PROGRAM FOR THE MULTINATIONAL CORPORATION

Sylvia B. Odenwald

Co-published with the American Society for Training and Development
Shows how to research, develop, and implement a comprehensive, customized training program that addresses the unique needs of a multinational work force. (225 pages)
ISBN: 1–55623–986–6

MANAGING DIVERSITY

A COMPLETE DESK REFERENCE AND PLANNING GUIDE

Lee Gardenswartz and Anita Rowe

Co-published with Pfeiffer & Company

This manager's handbook is filled with dozens of planning worksheets and activities designed to encourage high performance levels from diverse employees and cross-cultural teams. Includes creative approaches for mentoring, motivating, and training the work force. (446 pages)
ISBN: 1–55623–639–5

Also available in fine bookstores and libraries everywhere.